Cultural Atlas for Young People

ANCIENT ROME

Mike Corbishley

Facts On File

New York • Oxford

Managing Editor: Lionel Bender
Art Editor: Ben White
Designer: Malcolm Smythe
Text Editor: Miles Litvinoff
Assistant Editor: Madeleine Samuel
Project Editor: Graham Speake
Cartographic Editor: Olive Pearson
Design Consultant: John Ridgeway
Production: Clive Sparling and Catherine Moss

Advisory Editor of the series: Gillian Evans,
Fitzwilliam College, Cambridge
Advisory Editors for this volume: Tim Cornell,
University College London, John Matthews,
Queen's College, Oxford

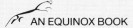 AN EQUINOX BOOK

Planned and produced by:
Equinox (Oxford) Ltd,
Musterlin House,
Jordan Hill Road, Oxford,
England OX2 8DP

Prepared by Lionheart Books

Media conversion and typesetting:
Peter MacDonald, Vanessa Hersey
and Una Macnamara

Copyright © Equinox (Oxford) Ltd 1989

Library of Congress Cataloging in Publication
Data

Corbishley, Mike
Cultural atlas for young people. Ancient
Rome/Mike Corbishley
96p. 300x235cm.
Includes index.
Summary: Text, maps, illustrations, charts,
tables, and chronologies depict the history,
society, and political life of ancient Rome and its
vast empire.

ISBN 0-8160-1970-3
1. Rome--History--Juvenile literature. 2. Rome--
Description and travel--Juvenile literature.
[1. Rome.] I. Title.
DG209.C68   1989   937--dc19

Published in North America by
Facts On File, Inc.
460 Park Avenue South
New York, N.Y. 10016

Origination by J. Film Process

Third Printing

Printed in Italy

Artwork and Picture Credits
Maps drawn by Lovell Johns, Oxford; Alan Mais, Hornchurch;
Location Map Services, Fleet; Thames Cartographic
Services, Maidenhead. All site plans by John Brennan,
Oxford.
Color artwork by Kevin Maddison and Chris Forsey; other
artwork by Peter Chesterton.
Abbreviations: t = top, c = center, b = bottom, l = left,
r = right etc.
1 Robert Harding Associates. 5 ZEFA. 8/9 Mauro Pucciarelli,
Rome. 10bl Mauro Pucciarelli, Rome. 12 Scala, Florence. 13l
Leonard von Matt. 13r Conrad Helbig, Zefa. 14tr John Fuller,
Cambridge. 14cr Alinari. 15 Giraudon. 16 Scala, Florence.
18tr German Archaeological Institute, Rome. 21tr Mauro
Pucciarelli, Rome. 24t German Archaelogical Institute, Rome.
24bl Sonia Halliday, Weston Turville. 25tl Mario Gerardi
Rome. 25tr Ray Gardner, London. 25b Mario Gerardi, Rome.
26tl, 26tr, 26cr Ilse Schneider-Lengyel, Phaidon archive,
Oxford. 26bl Alan Hutchison Library, London. 26/27 Alinari.
27t Leonard von Matt. 27c Alinari. 28/29 Mauro Pucciarelli,
Rome. 29t Malcolm Smythe. 29r Ronald Sheridan, London.
30 Ilse Schneider–Lengyel, Phaidon Archive, Oxford. 31
Mauro Pucciarelli, Rome. 32l John Fuller, Cambridge. 32r
Mario Gerardi, Rome. 34l Jean Roubier, Paris. 34r Elsevier
Archive, Amsterdam. 36bl Hirmer Fotoarchiv, Munich. 36tr
Alinari. 36cr Ray Gardner. 36br German Archaeological
Institute, Rome. 37t Ray Gardner. 37b Scala. 38tr Michael
Holford. 38cr Scala, Florence. 38bl Ronald Sheridan,
London. 38/39 Louvre, Paris. 39t Royal Commission on
Historical Monuments. 39c A.A.M. van der Heyden,
Amsterdam. 41r Michael Holford, Loughton. 42l Mario
Gerardi, Rome. 44l Roger Wood, London. 44r Museo della
Civiltà Romana. 46b, 46t Michael Dixon, Dover. 47 Michael
Vickers, Oxford. 48/49 Hayward Art Group. 50/51 Sheridan

Photo Library. 52t Brian Brake, John Hillelson Agency,
London. 52br Bernard Regent, Alan Hutchison Library,
London. 53t, 53b Sonia Halliday, Weston Turville. 54t Michael
Vickers, Oxford. 54b Roger Wood, London. 55t Elsevier
Archive, Amsterdam. 55b Alan Hutchison Library, London. 56
Brian Brake, John Hillelson Agency, London. 57 Scala,
Florence. 60cl Michael Holford. 60cr Rheinisches
Landesmuseum, Trier. 60bl Klaus Kerth, Zefa. 62t Roger
Agache, Service des Fouilles, Abbeville. 62b Dick Barnard,
Milverton. 63tr Photo Elsevier Archive. 63cl Heberden Coin
Room, Ashmolean Museum, Oxford. 63cr Bildarchiv Foto
Marburg. 63bl Aerofilms, Boreham Wood. 63br Rheinisches
Landesmuseum, Trier. 64t A.F. Kersting, London. 65 Dick
Barnard, Milverton, Somerset. 66t British Museum, London.
66b Michael Holford. 68/69 Brian Brake, John Hillelson
Agency, London. 70 Cambridge University Collection. 71t
Sussex Archaeological Society. 71b Sunday Times, London.
72t Scala. 72b Michael Holford. 75 Lothar Beckel, Bad Ischl,
Austria. 76t Michael Dixon, Dover. 76bl Sonia Halliday, Weston
Turville. 76br Nikos Kontos, Athens. 78tr Photoresources,
Dover. 78bl Ronald Sheridan, London. 78br the late Edwin
Smith. 79t Graham Speake, Oxford. 80bl Michael Dixon,
Dover. 82tr W. Wilkinson, London. 82cl Michael Dixon,
Dover. 82bl Sonia Halliday, Weston Turville. 83 Davil Brill, (C)
National Geographic Society. 84bl Rouen Museum. 84br
Robert Harding Associates, London. 86t Ronald Sheridan,
London. 86c R.D. Wilkinson, London. 86b Mrs Seton Lloyd,
reproduced from J.B. Segal, *Edessa the Blessed City* by
permission of Thames & Hudson. 87 Research Collections,
Princeton University. 88 Sonia Halliday, Weston Turville. 89bl
W. Brann, Zefa. 89r Sonia Halliday, Weston Turville. 90b
Florence Archaeological Museum (Photoresources). 90/91
Leonard von Matt, Buochs.

CONTENTS

INTRODUCTION

This book is about the Romans. It will help you step back 2,000 years and look at their world. The Romans were renowned for their buildings and feats of engineering. Nowadays we have motor-powered machinery to do most of the construction work for us. The Romans did invent machinery and were able to survey and draw accurate plans. However, we can still wonder at their determination to build, for example, a race track 650 yards long for chariots which could hold 350,000 spectators (Rome's Circus Maximus).

Writing and literature were introduced into all of the regions that became part of their Empire. The Latin language was soon being used throughout the Roman world. People used it for business and legal transactions. They were also able to enjoy plays at the theater and books – stories, histories and poems. A great deal of Roman literature has survived because it was copied by monks in the Middle Ages from ancient originals.

An important difference between the Roman Empire and most countries today is the large number of nations who lived there. There were about 60 million people living in the Roman Empire, at its biggest. These were people who had been brought into the Roman world – often by conquest. These "new" Romans usually thought of themselves as Roman – certainly they were encouraged to do so and to learn to use the standard language, Latin.

In many ways you could say that the Roman state was founded on slavery. Certainly there were large numbers of slaves owned throughout the Empire, on farms, in industries and in homes. Many of them were badly treated, but most were well cared for by their masters and mistresses, just as many servants were in the last century.

The Roman world was large, and it covered a very long period of history. The Romans taught their children that the city of Rome had been founded in 753 BC; their Empire in the West was taken over by German armies in AD 476. So Rome and a Roman way of life were important for over a thousand years.

Ancient Rome is divided into two main sections. The first, **The History of an Empire**, builds up the story of the Romans and tells how they gradually became the most important power in the world. Throughout this section there are maps illustrating specific themes or topics in the main text. Many of these maps are accompanied by charts giving important dates and events in Roman history. The second part, **The Geography of an Empire**, looks at the effect the Romans had on the lands they took over. The maps in this section are more typically atlas-like, containing details of rivers, towns, roads, mountains and lowlands. Important Roman towns and villages, with their modern and Latin names, can be located using the Gazetteer on pages 93-94.

The book is called an atlas – and that is what it is. It is full of maps to help you understand the story and to see where places and events were. You might like to compare these maps with those in a modern atlas to see how things have changed. Our story is arranged in double-page spreads. Each spread is a complete story. So you can read the book from beginning to end, or just dip into it to learn about a specific topic. The Glossary on page 92 contains definitions of historical and Roman terms used in the book.

Abbreviations used in this book
AD = Anno Domini (the year of the Lord; of the Christian era).
BC = Before Christ. c. = circa (about). in = inch. ft = foot.
mi = mile.
When referring to dates, early 3rd century BC, for example, means about 290 or 280 BC, and late 3rd century BC means about 220 or 210 BC.

▷ The Triumphal Arch of Septimius Severus in the Roman Forum.

TABLE OF DATES

	800 BC	600 BC	500 BC	400 BC	300 BC	200 BC
ROME AND ITALY	Foundation of Rome 753 Tarquin I 616-579 Growth of the city	Servius Tullius 579-534 Reorganization of the tribes, army and constitution Tarquin II 534-509 Beginning of the Republic 509 Rome most important town in Latium	Latins defeated at Lake Regillus 499 Invasions of Sabines, Aequi and Volsci Domination of the patricians Campania overrun by Samnites 420 Siege and capture of Veii 405-396	Rome sacked by Gauls Latin War 340 Campania incorporated in Roman state 338 Roman colonization and conquest of Italy 334-264 Second Samnite War 327-304	Third Samnite War 298-290 Pyrrhus' invasion 280-275 Early Roman coinage (from c. 280) First War with Carthage 264-241 Gauls invade Italy 225 Second War with Carthage 218-202	Direct taxation on Roman citizens abolished 167 Defeat of Cimbri and Teutones 102-101

Villanovan hut urn c. 800 BC

Head of Apollo from Veii, c. 500 BC

The Capitoline wolf, early 5th century BC

Coin of Hannibal c. 210 BC

ART AND ARCHITECTURE	Primitive huts on the Palatine Rich tombs at Caere, Praeneste etc. Roman Forum laid out; first permanent stone buildings in Rome	Temples of Diana, Fortuna and Mater Matuta c. 560 Walls of Servius Tullius Temple of Jupiter Capitolinus 509 Etruscan tomb paintings	Temple of Saturn 497 Temple of Ceres 493 Temple of Castor 484 Temple of Apollo 431	Walls around Rome rebuilt 378 Via Appia, Aqua Appia built 312	Program of temple building in Rome 302-272 Roman fine pottery industry flourishes Circus Flaminius 221	Greek art brought to Rome 200- Basilica Porcia built in the Roman Forum 184 Basilica Aemilia and Aemilian bridge 179 Temple of Fortuna at Praeneste c. 120

Cylindrical "cist" (container) c. 650 BC

The "Lapis Niger", Rome's oldest public document c. 500 BC

The circular temple in the Forum Boarium late 2nd century BC

LATIN LITERATURE		Earliest Latin inscriptions c. 600	The Twelve Tables of Roman laws written 451-450		Appius Claudius Caecus, politician Livius Andronicus, Naevius, Plautus, Ennius, Statius Caecilius and Pacuvius, playwrights and poets Cato, historian, scholar	Terence and Accius, playwrights L. Calpurnius Piso and Caelius Antipater, historians C. Gracchus, L. Crassus and Q. Hortensius, lawyers and politicians

100 BC	AD	AD 100	AD 200	AD 300	AD 400	AD 500
War with allies 91-89 Civil War: Sulla dictator 83-82 Revolt of Spartacus 73-71 Civil War: Caesar dictator 49-44 Murder of Caesar 44 Reign of Octavian/ Augustus 31 BC- AD 14	Fire of Rome 64 Eruption of Vesuvius 79	Antonine emperors 117-93	Roman citizenship extended to all free inhabitants of the provinces 212	"Great Persecution" of Christians 303-05 Freedom of worship restored 313 Constantine sole ruler of the Empire 324-37 Division of the Empire 395	Imperial court shifted to Ravenna 402 Visigoths under Alaric sack Rome 410 Rome pillaged by Vandals 455 Last Roman emperor of the west 476 Barbarian kings at Ravenna 476-540	Byzantine reconquest of Italy 540

Augustus as high priest, late 1st century BC

The Colosseum, AD 79

Diocletian and Maximian, c. AD 300

Mosaic of Justinian at Ravenna, c. AD 560

100 BC	AD	AD 100	AD 200	AD 300	AD 400	AD 500
Record office 78 Theater of Pompey 55 Forum of Caesar 46 Arch of Augustus 21 Baths of Agrippa 19 Theater of Marcellus 17 Forum of Augustus 2	Augustan building program at Rome Colosseum dedicated 79	Trajan's Forum dedicated 112 Pantheon rebuilt 118-28 Hadrian's Villa at Tivoli 126-34	Severan building at Leptis Magna Baths of Caracalla built at Rome 216 Aurelian builds walls around Rome 271	Arch of Constantine Church-building programs at Rome, Jerusalem and Constantinople	Mosaics in churches at Ravenna	St Sophia rebuilt at Constantinople 537

The triumphal arch of Saintes

The "pastor bonus" (Good Shepherd) sarcophagus, early 4th century

Gold buckle from the Thetford treasure, Norfolk, late 4th century

100 BC	AD	AD 100	AD 200	AD 300	AD 400	AD 500
Cicero, lawyer, philosopher Caesar, lawyer, historian Lucretius, poet and philosopher Sallust and Livy, historians Catullus, Virgil, Horace, Tibullus, Propertius, Ovid, poets	Seneca the Elder, orator Persius, Lucan, Martial, poets Pliny the Elder, natural historian Pliny the Younger, letter writer Tacitus, historian	Juvenal, poet Suetonius, historian Apuleius, novelist	Ulpian, Papinian, lawyers Tertullian, Christian writer	Ausonius and Claudian, poets Ambrose, Jerome and Augustine, Christian writers Symmachus, orator Ammianus Marcellinus, historian	Jerome translates Old Testament into Latin c. 404 Orosius, historian Servius and Macrobius, scholars Theodosian code compiled 429/37 Sidonius Apollinaris, poet	Boethius, philosopher Cassiodorus, historian and administrator

PART ONE

THE HISTORY OF AN EMPIRE

△ Hannibal leading his army across the Alps to attack the Romans in 218 BC – from a central Italian plate.

▷ Tiber island, Rome, with the ruins of the Pons Aemilius (2nd century BC) in the foreground.

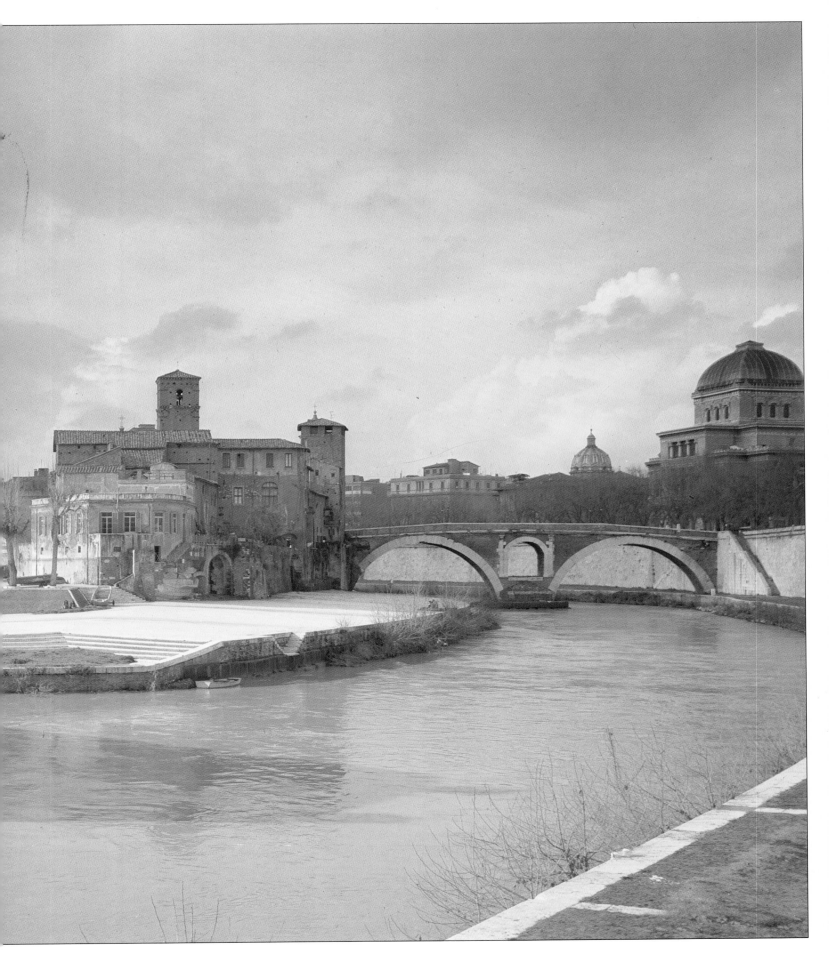

A LAND CALLED ITALY

"Beyond the foothill of the Alps you reach the beginning of what is now called Italy." This is what the geographer Strabo wrote in the time of the first emperor, Augustus.

The name Italy comes from the word used by the Romans: *Italia*. But it is probably even older than that; we think it comes from a word the Greeks used, pronounced *witalia*, meaning "the land of cattle". This book is not just about a "land of cattle" but about a huge empire which stretched from the North Sea to the Black Sea and from the Atlas mountains in North Africa to the river Danube in central Europe.

Varied landscape

The story of Rome and its Empire begins with the land of Italy. It is a large country made up of different landscapes. A mountain range running north and south, the Apennines, divides the country like a backbone.

On the eastern side there is little room between these mountains and the sea. There are few natural harbors, and the soil is poor. The western side has a better climate, with a great deal of land suitable for farming. This was the side most people wanted to settle in.

Rivers of Italy

The Tiber and the Arno rivers were very important in the history of the first people who settled in Italy. The plains around the rivers were good farming land, and the rivers themselves were used as main routes inland. The western side of Italy also has more rainfall than the east and good harbors.

In northern Italy, south of the Alps lies a huge plain with the river Po running for 350mi through it. The river brings down silt which helps make the soil fertile. The marshy land this produced on the coast of the Adriatic Sea was reclaimed during the Roman period by earth walls and drainage canals.

Rich in resources

Italy was much more wooded in early times than it is today. There were forests of larch and maple on the slopes of the Alps, and the area around Rome produced pine and beech. There was always plenty of good stone for building, as well as clay for making bricks and tiles and for pottery. The farming land was suitable for all sorts of animals – cattle, sheep, goats and horses. The Romans grew a variety of crops such as wheat, vegetables, grapes for wine and olives for eating and for their oil.

The people of Italy

The people who came to this fertile land were from all over the Mediterranean and beyond. Celtic-speaking Gauls came from beyond the Alps, and Greeks settled on the southern coasts and in Sicily, calling the land Magna Graecia ("Great Greece").

Over the centuries the Romans took over more and more neighboring countries. Eventually all the peoples in these lands became "Roman". For example, the Emperor Diocletian came from the far-off province of Dalmatia, now Yugoslavia; and the poet Martial thought of himself as a Roman even though he was born in what we now call Spain.

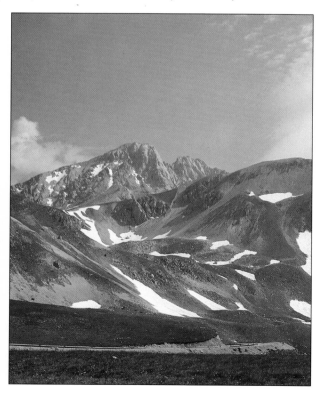

▽ The Gran Sasso (the "Great Crag") mountain. At 9,900ft it dominates the Apennines in central Italy and is the highest point in the peninsula.

▷ Only about one-fifth of Italy is flat plain. The rest is mountainous or hilly. Northern Italy shares its climate with central Europe, while the southern climate is typically Mediterranean.

SWITZERLAN
Rhône
Matterhorn 14688
Mt Blanc 15771
VALL D'AOS
FRANCE
PIEMON
LIG
MONA

Feet
6500
3250
650
0

■ Capital city
△ 12792 Mountain peak (feet)
–·–·– International boundary
– – – Regional boundary
Scale 1:4 250 000

0   150k
0   100

ALGERIA A

Rhine
ALPS
AUSTRIA
△Ortles
3899
DOLOMITES
TRENTINO—
ALTO ADIGE
FRIULI —
VENEZIA
GIULIA
L di Como
LOMBARDIA
6
L Maggiore
Bergamo
L d'Iseo
L di Garda Vicenza
Piave
Trieste
Milan
Brescia
Verona
Venice
Ticino
Padua
Venice
Gulf of
VENEZIA
EUGANEA
Venice
Adige
5
Trebbia
Piacenza
Po
Parma
Ferrara
Reno
JURIAN ALPS
oa
Bologna
Ravenna
EMILIA —
ROMAGNA
Ronco
Forli
Rimini
La Spezia
Pisa
Arno
Florence
SAN
MARINO
Ancona
ITALY
Ligurian
Sea
Arezzo
MARCHE
TOSCANA
APENNINES
Elba
L Trasimeno
Ombrone
△
Mt Amiata
1738
Perugia
Golo
Tuscan
Archipelago
UMBRIA
Terni
Mt Corno
△2914
Adriatic Sea
4
Corsica
(FRANCE)
L di
Bolsena
Tiber
Pescara
L di
Bracciano
Amaro
△2795
Strait of
Bonifacio
■
Rome
ABRUZZO
Sangro
Prom.Del
Gargano
Sacco
LAZIO
MOLISE
Travoliere
Tiranë ■
Volturno
Foggia
Della Puglia
Ofanto
Bari
ALBANIA
3
CAMPANIA
PUGLIA
ari
Naples
Mt Vesuvius
△ 1277
MURGE
Brindisi
Salerno
BASILICATA
Taranto
Capri
Agri
Strait of
Otranto
Sardinia
Panagro
Gulf of
Taranto
Crati
Corfu
(GREECE)
Tyrrhenian Sea
CALABRIA
2
Cagliari
Ionian Sea
Lipari
Islands
Ustica
Mediterranean Sea
Egadi
Palermo
Messina
Reggio di Calabria
Sicily
Mt Etna △
3323
Strait of
Messina
Sicilian Channel
Catania
1
Salso
TUNISIA
Pantelleria
B
C
D
E
■
Tunis

THE MYSTERIOUS ETRUSCANS

Centuries before the Romans, the area north of Rome, called Etruria, was home to the Etruscans. The Romans themselves liked to believe that their country was founded by warrior heroes who were descended from the gods. But some Roman and Greek writers tried to investigate the earlier peoples of the region and were very curious about these Etruscans.

The Etruscan people gradually developed their way of life in this hilly but fertile region of west-central Italy. By the 7th century BC they had formed themselves into 12 states. Each state was like an independent country, with its own capital city, but they were all Etruscan.

Together the Etruscan states began to conquer other territories around them. By the 6th century BC there were Etruscan cities as far north as Mantua and as far south as Salerno.

A rich and powerful people

The Etruscans became wealthy through agriculture, through trade with the Greeks and other peoples and because they developed industries such as metalworking and pottery. They built large cities which were laid out with roads and sewage and water systems.

In fact, many of the ideas we think of as Roman were invented by the Etruscans. For example, the Etruscans developed a system to bring water into their cities by aqueducts. The name for Rome was originally an Etruscan word: Roma.

Lost language

One of the reasons we know far less about the Etruscans than we do about the later Romans is because of their language. There were people still speaking Etruscan in the 2nd century AD, but the language was lost after that. Only a few inscriptions survive today.

Most of our recorded information about Etruscan customs and beliefs consists of the statements of Greek and Roman writers, who were often uneducated or prejudiced.

Etruscan tombs and art

We do have plenty of evidence about the Etruscans from the decorated underground tombs built for the rich. The cemeteries were in special areas outside the cities. Skillful architects, builders and artists were employed to

◁ Tomb portrait from Tarquinia. Many of the tombs were covered with beautiful wall paintings. From an inscription we know that this lady with an elaborate hair-style is called Velia.

▽ Major Etruscan cities in the 6th century BC. The Etruscan civilization developed between the rivers Arno and Tiber, west of the Apennines.

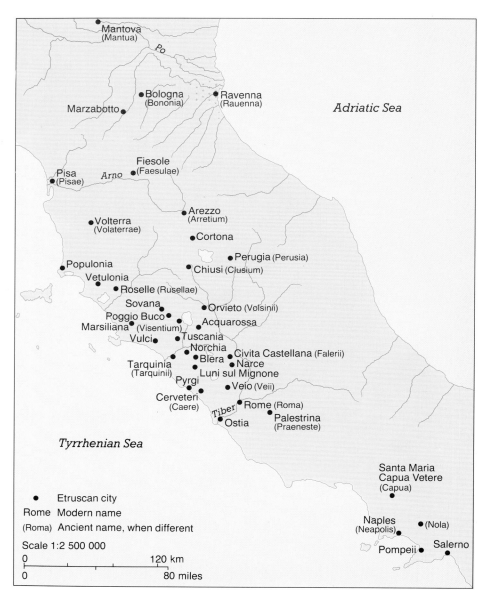

Mantova (Mantua)

Po

Bologna (Bononia) Ravenna (Rauenna)

Marzabotto

Adriatic Sea

Pisa (Pisae) Arno Fiesole (Faesulae)

Volterra (Volaterrae) Arezzo (Arretium)

Cortona

Perugia (Perusia)

Populonia Chiusi (Clusium)

Vetulonia

Roselle (Rusellae)

Sovana Orvieto (Volsinii)

Poggio Buco Acquarossa

Marsiliana (Visentium)

Vulci Tuscania

Norchia Civita Castellana (Falerii)

Blera Narce

Tarquinia (Tarquinii) Luni sul Mignone

Pyrgi Veio (Veii)

Cerveteri (Caere) Tiber Rome (Roma)

Ostia Palestrina (Praeneste)

Tyrrhenian Sea

Santa Maria Capua Vetere (Capua)

● Etruscan city
Rome Modern name
(Roma) Ancient name, when different

Scale 1:2 500 000

0 ———————— 120 km
0 ———————— 80 miles

Naples (Neapolis) (Nola)

Pompeii Salerno

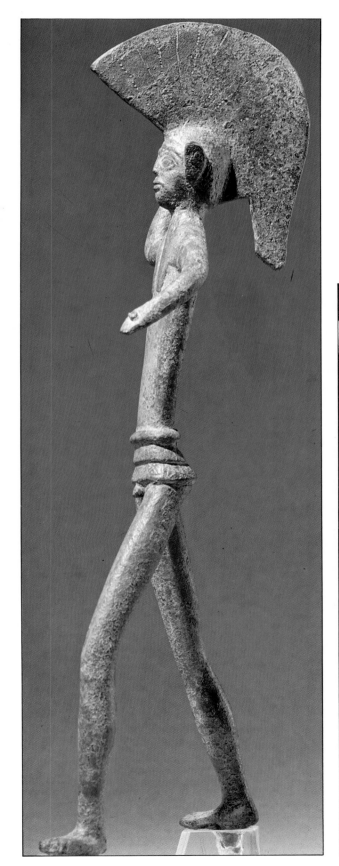

◁ The Etruscans were skilled metalworkers, especially in bronze. This statue of a warrior was one of the objects placed in an underground tomb.

▽ This tomb in Caere shows what part of an Etruscan house would have looked like, including couch, chair and shields on the walls.

create these tombs. Below ground the tombs are built like houses for the dead, complete with furniture. Above ground the great mounds of earth that mark them, many feet high, often still survive.

The Etruscans believed that there was another life following death. People were buried in ceremonial style, with food for the next world. A large number of objects were also placed in these tombs – jewelry, statues and vases, for example.

Today these fine Etruscan tombs are still under threat from treasure-hunters who break in and steal the fine artwork and sell it abroad for high prices.

THE BEGINNINGS OF ROME

Although the Etruscans were powerful and conquered territory in central Italy, they were not the only people who lived there. Other tribes were the Samnites, Umbrians, Sabines and Latins. In the city of Roma – Rome – the Latins were the largest group.

The Latin language

Latin was the language spoken by the Latins who lived in the plain around, and to the south of, Rome. Latin probably arrived from across the Alps before the 8th century BC.

As the Roman state became bigger, the language spread to millions of people across the Roman world. From there Latin has passed into many European languages. Here are some examples from English with the Latin in brackets: civilian (*civis*, a citizen of a town), mile (*mille passuum*, a thousand paces), family (*familia*) and second (*secundus*).

Romulus, Remus and early kings

The Romans believed that Romulus, the first ruler (they called him *rex* or king), founded the city on April 21 in the year 753 BC. Roman children were all told how Romulus and his twin brother Remus were cast adrift in a basket on the river Tiber by the wicked brother of their step-grandfather. They were saved by a she-wolf and grew up to found Rome. Romulus killed his brother Remus in an argument, according to the story.

The site of the city had advantages: a good river crossing, plenty of fresh water and pleasant surrounding hills. Years later a writer described the setting as ideal "for a city destined to grow great".

Whether or not Romulus really existed and became a Roman king, we do know that the first rulers of Rome came from both the Etruscans and the Latins. The first three, so inscriptions and records tell us, were Numa Pompilius (a Sabine), Tullus Hostilius (a Latin) and Ancus Martius (a Sabine).

These were followed by three Etruscan kings: Lucius Tarquinius Priscus, Servius Tullius and Lucius Tarquinius. The last one was nicknamed The Proud. The people of Rome hated him and his arrogant rule. They threw him out and established a completely different form of government for themselves.

△ The "Capitoline Wolf". The she-wolf kept Romulus and Remus alive by suckling them. This bronze statue of the she-wolf was made by an Etruscan artist in the 6th century BC. The twins were added in the early 16th century AD, but it is likely that there were others there originally.

◁ This Roman symbol was borrowed from the Etruscans. The axe and bundle of rods represented the power of consuls.

▽ Rome's allies and colonies. Allies supplied troops. Colonies were set up by Roman citizens.

290 BC
Key as map opposite
Scale 1:3 000 000

0 — 100 km
0 — 50 miles

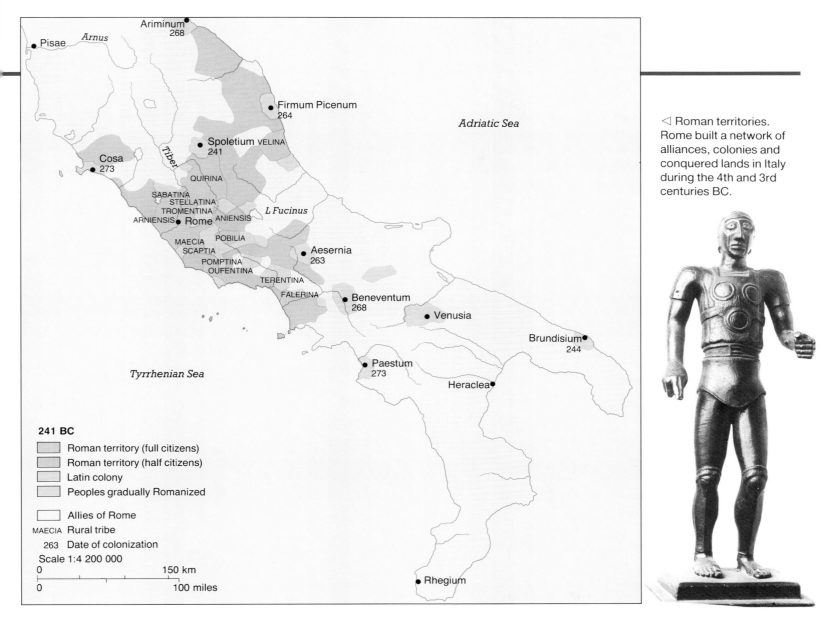

Firmum Picenum
264

Adriatic Sea

Spoletium VELINA
241

Cosa
273

Tiber

QUIRINA

SABATINA
STELLATINA
TROMENTINA
ARNIENSIS• Rome ANIENSIS

L Fucinus

MAECIA POBILIA
SCAPTIA

POMPTINA
OUFENTINA

Aesernia
263

TERENTINA

FALERINA   Beneventum
268

Venusia

Brundisium•
244

Paestum
273

Tyrrhenian Sea

Heraclea•

241 BC

☐ Roman territory (full citizens)
☐ Roman territory (half citizens)
☐ Latin colony
☐ Peoples gradually Romanized

☐ Allies of Rome
MAECIA Rural tribe
263 Date of colonization
Scale 1:4 200 000
0   150 km
0   100 miles

Rhegium•

▷ Roman territories. Rome built a network of alliances, colonies and conquered lands in Italy during the 4th and 3rd centuries BC.

Government by elections

The Romans called their new form of government *respublica* (our word "republic"). It literally meant "a matter for the people", and that was what the government was. Each year two officials called consuls were elected by the citizens.

Consuls had much the same power as kings and were heads of government and in charge of the army. However, they were in office for only a year and had to agree with each other about what to do.

Other officials were brought in to do the other jobs of government. Praetors were chief judges; censors kept the register of citizens who could vote; quaestors looked after the state's finances; and aediles were in charge of all public works. The senate, made up of ex-officials, formed a parliament which discussed matters of state and advised the officials.

Citizens and conquest

The Roman people were divided into "classes". The patricians were the noble families who traced their origins back to early Rome. The plebeians were the ordinary working people. They could vote but could not hold high office such as the consulship. Later a new class emerged, the *equites* ("knights"), who were property-owning business men.

Although the state was a republic, and the system of government was democracy, not everyone could vote: slaves and women were excluded.

At first the new Roman state had friendly relations with its neighbors. Gradually, though, the Romans forced them to become part of their state – sometimes simply by conquering them. In this way a pattern of expansion began that would produce one of the world's greatest empires.

△ A Samnite warrior from the 6th or 5th century BC. He is fully protected with chest and leg armor. The Romans copied the idea of the long rectangular shield from these Samnites.

15

WAR WITH CARTHAGE

The Roman republic went from strength to strength. Rome's armies conquered all of Italy, defeated the Greek King Pyrrhus in 275 BC and became a major force to be reckoned with in the Mediterranean. But they were not the only "world power" there.

The Carthaginians' territory covered North Africa and part of Spain. Carthage then began to conquer Sicily, the large island close to the "toe" of Italy.

▷ *"The elephants were of great use to the Carthaginians. The enemy were too terrified of their appearance to come anywhere near them"* – Polybius, Roman historian.

Battles between Rome and Carthage

First war
264 BC Carthage occupies Messana. Romans defeat the Carthaginians and occupy the town.
260 BC Rome builds its fleet. Full-scale war.
241 BC Carthage surrenders.

Second war
221 BC Hannibal made commander-in-chief.
219 BC Saguntum captured. Rome declares war.
218 BC Hannibal marches across the Alps. Romans defeated at rivers Ticino and Trebia.
217 BC Two Roman legions lost at Lake Trasimeno.
216 BC Rome's worst defeat, at Cannae.
204 BC Romans invade North Africa.
202 BC Carthage defeated at Zama.
183 BC Hannibal commits suicide.

Third war
149 BC War breaks out again.
146 BC City of Carthage completely destroyed. North Africa becomes a Roman province.

The first war

When the Carthaginians occupied the town of Messana (modern Messina) the Romans sent two legions of soldiers there and defeated them. Full-scale war then broke out. For 20 years the two mighty nations fought each other. A few years later the Romans moved into Corsica and Sardinia. The war ended in 241 BC with a battle off the west coast of Sicily. Rome occupied Sicily and made it its first province.

Hannibal – enemy of Rome

Hamilcar had been the Carthaginian commander at the end of the first war against Rome. In 237 BC he led an army into Spain to conquer new territory and defend Carthaginian settlements already there. Spain provided the Carthaginians with rich supplies of farm

ATLANTIC OCEAN

Douro
Tagus
Garonne
Arausi
Tolosa • NARBONENSIS
Narbo • Mas
Ebro
Numantia
Emporia
CELTIBERIA   Tarraco
Der tosa
LUSITANIA
Saguntum
HISPANIA
HISPANIA   Baecula
BALEARES
Ilipa   HISPANIA
Baetis *Guadalquivir*   CITERIOR
ULTERIOR
Gades
Carthago Nova

→ Carthaginian army
→ Roman army
☐ Area of Carthaginian rule, 218 BC
☐ Area of Roman rule, 218 BC
✕ Major battle
● Roman base outside area of Roman rule
Scale 1:10 000 000
0   600 km
0   400 miles

▽ Campaign routes of the two "world powers". Both the Romans and the Carthaginians needed an efficient navy. At first the Carthaginians had the naval advantage. Both sides also needed wealth to pay for the expensive wars and for their allies.

◁ The Carthaginians were a seafaring trading nation with a large navy. The Romans had to build a fleet especially to fight them. First they built 120 ships such as these, later another 200. Off the Aegates Islands west of Sicily the Romans sank 50 Carthaginian warships laden with supplies for the troops and captured 70 more. The rest of the fleet escaped, but Carthage was beaten.

Ticino
Mediolanum
Cremona
Trebia ✕ Placentia
Po
Pisae
✕ Metaurus
✕ L Trasimeno
CORSICA
Tiber
● Rome
●Ostia
Cannae ✕
●Capua
Brundisium ●
●Tarentum
●Lissus
Apollonia
MACEDONIA
SARDINIA
●Croton
Messana
Rhegium
Aegates Is
●Lilybaeum
SICILIA
● Syracusae
Utica ●
Carthage
✕Zama
Hadrumetum ●
⊂ Melita

Mediterranean Sea

produce and metals with which they fed and equipped their armies.

"Hamilcar was about to cross to Spain with his army and was making sacrifices. Hannibal, then about nine years old, was childishly teasing his father to take him too. His father, still angry at the loss of Sicily and Sardinia, led him to the altar and made him swear to be the enemy of Rome as soon as he was able" – the historian Livy.

Hamilcar's son, Hannibal, took over control of Carthaginian forces in Spain in 221 BC. He was only 25 years old. After two years he conquered the town of Saguntum, Rome's ally. The Romans sent two armies against the Carthaginians – one to Carthage, and the other to Massilia (now Marseille).

Crossing the Alps
Hannibal astonished the Romans by marching to Italy across the Alps. No Roman believed he would take this route. His huge army of 40,000 men also had 37 war elephants with them. It was a hard march, and Hannibal reached Italy with only 26,000 men and 12 elephants. However, he brought in more troops and with an army of about 50,000 began to defeat the Romans in their own country.

Rome saved
A new Roman general, Publius Cornelius Scipio, was appointed to cope with this crisis. He went to attack Carthage and forced Hannibal to fight him there. Hannibal's army was defeated at Zama in 202 BC.

THE LEGIONS

The Romans needed a large army to conquer all the areas they wanted to rule and to defeat enemies such as Hannibal.

At first the Roman soldiers were part-time. Men were called up for duty whenever an army was needed. Not every man was called. Only Roman citizens between the ages of 17 and 46 who owned some property could be soldiers. Later in the history of Rome men volunteered to become full-time soldiers and sailors and served at least 20 years.

Army organization

Over the years the way in which the army fought gradually changed. New tactics were invented or copied from other armies. The soldiers were organized into large units called legions. Soldiers were known as legionaries. For marching, training and fighting, the soldiers operated in smaller groups of about a hundred, commanded by a centurion. (The English word "century", meaning 100, comes from the Latin word.)

△ Roman soldiers battling with tribesmen of Dacia in the 2nd century AD. Notice how well armed and protected the Romans are, with their helmets and armor.

A legionary's load
A legionary carried about 66lb of kit on the march. It included tools for building camp, bags to hold a saw, chain, rope and provisions, pots and pans for cooking and a leather shield cover.

Soldiers were trained not only to fight but also to build the forts and roads needed to hold conquered territory.

Weapons and uniform

Roman soldiers fought with long spears and swords. Over the years their uniform and armor changed. In the early years of Rome a legionary often wore a helmet with long plumes of feathers, carried an oval-shaped shield and was protected by a short suit of chain mail.

Later the shape of the shield changed, and the full-time soldier in the 2nd century AD had plates of metal joined together into armor to protect his upper body. A legionary's helmet now had flaps to protect his cheeks and neck.

△ When preparing for battle, soldiers equipped with swords and spears would form protective ranks in front of cavalry and archers.

◁ This soldier is fully equipped for a march. In addition to the items shown (far left) he carried rations for three days.

△ On a march through enemy territory, the army would build a camp each night, strongly fortified by banks and wooden walls.

△ In the foreground stands a centurion, the leader of a small army group. Beside him is a *signifer* who carried the group's standard or emblem, the *signum*.

EARLY YEARS OF CRISIS

In the 2nd century BC there was a serious threat to Rome on its northern and eastern borders. The northern tribes – Cimbri, Teutones and Ambrones – made Spain, southern Gaul and even Italy unsafe. In 105 BC a whole Roman army was slaughtered at Arausio by these northern warriors.

In the east Mithridates VI, King of Pontus, occupied Asia and the Greek islands. He was welcomed in the Roman territory of Asia in 88 BC, where the people had been treated badly by their Roman masters. Mithridates was defeated in 63 BC.

Another threat to Rome came from large bands of pirates who were based in the eastern Mediterranean. The Roman commander Pompey finally defeated them in 67 BC.

Unrest and hostility in the Empire

In the west and north
133 BC   After 70 years of war Rome finally defeats the local people at Numantia in Spain.
113 BC   Cimbri defeat Romans at Noreia.
105 BC   Roman army slaughtered at Arausio.
102 BC   Teutones defeated at Aquae Sextiae.
101 BC   Cimbri defeated at Vercellae.

In the east and Africa
146 BC   Corinth, capital city of Achaea in Greece, destroyed by the Romans.
133 BC   Roman province of Asia formed.
112 BC   War with Numidian King Jugurtha. Roman victory in **105 BC**.
88 BC   King Mithridates occupies Asia, but it is regained by the Roman general Sulla in **85 BC**.
86 BC   Sulla captures Athens for Rome.

Around Italy
136-132 and 104-101 BC   Slave uprisings in Sicily against the Romans.
126-122 and 115-111 BC   Revolts in Sardinia.
91-89 BC   War against rebellious allies in Italy.

▽ From 146 to 70 BC Rome faced difficulties throughout its Empire. The period of crisis ended only when ambitious men such as Marius, Sulla and Pompey became powerful.

Legend:
- Roman Empire, 100 BC
- Area ruled by Mithridates
- Area under influence of Mithridates
- Routes of Cimbri, Teutones and Ambrones
- Mithridates' army
- Pirate stonghold
- 241 Date of Roman acquisition
- ✗ Roman victory
- ✗ Roman defeat

Scale 1:15 000 000
0 ____ 500 km
0 ____ 400 miles

Map labels: Arno, ATLANTIC OCEAN, Loire, GALLIA, Cimbri, Teutones and Ambrones, Cimbri, Teutones and Ambrones travel to Arausio from Jutland and North Sea coast, Noreia 113, Sava, Vercellae 101, Rhône, Arausio 105, Burdigala, Aquae Sextiae 102, Numantia, Ebro, NARBONENSIS 121, Narbo, Massilia, Douro, CORSICA 227, ITALIA, Rome, Tagus, Saguntum, Dyrrhachium, Brundisium, Thessalonica, Dardar, MACEDONIA 146, Perg, HISPANIA CITERIOR 206–197, BALEARES, SARDINIA 238, Orchomenus, HISPANIA ULTERIOR 206–197, Chaeronea 86, 85, Athenae, Carthago Nova, ACHAEA, SICILIA 241, Carthago, Syracusae, NUMIDIA, AFRICA 146, Mediterranean Sea, PTOL

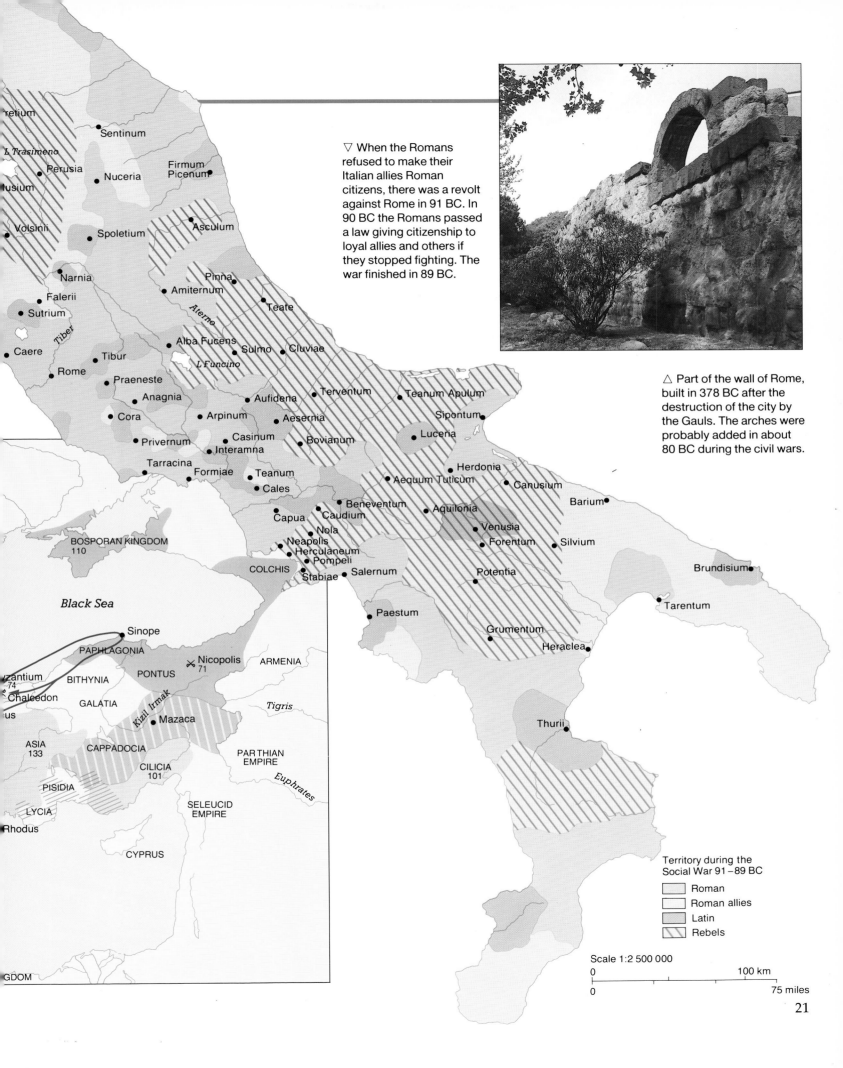

retium

Sentinum

L Trasimeno

lusium

Perusia   Nuceria

Firmum
Picenum

Volsinii   Spoletium   Asculum

Narnia   Pinna

Falerii   Amiternum

Sutrium   *Aterno*   Teate

Tiber

Caere   Alba Fucens   Sulmo   Cluviae

Tibur   *L Funcino*

Rome   Praeneste

Anagnia   Terventum   Teanum Apulum

Cora   Arpinum   Aesernia   Sipontum

Privernum   Casinum   Bovianum   Luceria

Interamna

Tarracina   Herdonia

Formiae   Teanum   Aequum Tuticum   Canusium

Cales   Barium

Beneventum   Aquilonia

Capua   Caudium

Nola   Venusia

Neapolis   Forentum   Silvium

Herculaneum

Pompeii   Potentia

COLCHIS   Salernum   Brundisium

Stabiae

BOSPORAN KINGDOM
110

Black Sea   Paestum   Tarentum

Grumentum

Sinope   Heraclea

PAPHLAGONIA

Nicopolis
71

yzantium   ARMENIA   Thurii

74   BITHYNIA   PONTUS

Chalcedon

us   GALATIA

Kizil Irmak   Mazaca

ASIA   *Tigris*
133

CAPPADOCIA

PISIDIA   CILICIA   PARTHIAN
101   EMPIRE

Euphrates

LYCIA

Rhodus   SELEUCID
EMPIRE

CYPRUS

▽ When the Romans
refused to make their
Italian allies Roman
citizens, there was a revolt
against Rome in 91 BC. In
90 BC the Romans passed
a law giving citizenship to
loyal allies and others if
they stopped fighting. The
war finished in 89 BC.

△ Part of the wall of Rome,
built in 378 BC after the
destruction of the city by
the Gauls. The arches were
probably added in about
80 BC during the civil wars.

Territory during the
Social War 91–89 BC

Roman

Roman allies

Latin

Rebels

Scale 1:2 500 000

0   100 km

0   75 miles

GDOM

21

REPUBLICAN ROME – GROWTH OF A CITY

The seven hills of Rome

As early as 1000 BC there were villages built on the seven hills which later made up the area of the capital city of the Roman state. Under Etruscan rule the villages became one community, the first town of Rome. The town grew, and the valleys which ran down to the river Tiber soon filled with buildings.

The river led to the sea, where the port of Ostia was established. The forum, Rome's trading and business center, was built in around 600 BC. About 378 BC a wall was built to enclose the area of Rome. This Servian Wall was originally thought to have been built by one of the early kings of Rome, Servius Tullius. The city was never formally planned out (unlike Republican Rome. The dotted line of the Aurelian Wall shows the city's extent by the late 3rd century AD. Details of the city's first stone theater (inset right), built by Pompey in 55 BC, survive on a marble plan of the city.

Hills of Rome

SERVIAN WALL

Tiber

Campus Martius

Temple of Quirinus

QUIRINALIS COLLIS

VIMINALIS COLLIS

CISPIUS MONS

Via Salaria

Via Nomentana

Via Collatina

Via Labicana

ESQUILIAE

OPPIUS MONS

AURELIAN WALL

Saepta Julia

Porticoes of Pompey

Theater of Pompey

Largo Argentina

Villa Publica

Temples of Apollo and Belona

Capitolium

Sacra Via

Via Aurelia

Bridge of Fabricius

Bridge of Cestius

Bridge of Aemilius

Bridge of Sublicius

PALATINUS MONS

Circus Maximus

CAELIUS MONS

Via Tusculana

Temple of Diana

Temple of Juno Regina

AVENTINUS MONS

Tiber

Porticus Aemilia

Via Ostiensis

Via Ardeatina

Via Appia

1   Temple of Juno Moneta
2   Tabularium
3   Basilica Aemilia
4   Temple of Jupiter Capitolinus
5   Basilica Julia
6   Temples of Fortuna and Mater Matuta
7   Temple of Portunus
8   Temple of Hercules Victor
9   Ara Maxima
10   Temple of Cybele or Magna Mater

0   500 meters
0   1500 feet

N

THEATRVM

later Roman towns, especially in the provinces) and it grew in a haphazard way.

Rome expands

Rome had around 100,000 inhabitants in the 3rd century BC. This number rose rapidly to nearly one million in Julius Caesar's time. Although the poor still lived in ramshackle accommodation in the valleys, the rich had moved to the cooler, healthier hills.

The huge population needed water in vast quantities. Many aqueducts were built to bring water to the heart of Rome. A network of roads was developed, providing main highways through the city and across Italy.

Public buildings

By the end of the 4th century BC, Rome had become an important and very wealthy town. Splendid buildings surrounded the first forum, and other public squares were built. The city center had a number of fine temples.

By the 1st century BC, 100,000 people could watch chariot racing in the Circus Maximus. Near the river and the market-places great warehouses and trading centers, such as the Porticus Aemilia, were built.

Not many of the monuments and buildings built during the Republic survive today. They were replaced by those erected under the emperors.

△ Great stone aqueducts were built to bring water into Rome from the hills. The water was carried in a channel on the top. Rome's first aqueduct was built by the politician Appius Claudius in 312 BC. It was called the Aqua Appia. The same man also built the Via Appia, a road from Rome to Capua.

THE RISE OF JULIUS CAESAR

Julius Caesar claimed that he was descended from the gods. He said that Aeneas, the Trojan hero and son of the goddess Venus, was his ancestor. Surviving records suggest that he was born between 102 and 100 BC into an important family of the patrician class. He was related by marriage to Marius, a politician and an enemy of the dictator Sulla during the civil war of 83 BC. This connection helped his career but it also brought him into conflict with Sulla.

A career in the state's service

Like so many other Roman aristocrats, Julius Caesar began his career in the army, serving in the eastern Empire. On his return to Rome he began his political career by taking various public offices, such as head of financial affairs in Spain. Later he was in charge of all public building in Rome, chief priest and a governor in Spain. Finally he was elected to the highest position as consul in 60 BC. For one year he shared, with a fellow consul, complete control of the government and army.

Conquest of Gaul

After his consulship Caesar went, in 58 BC, to govern the provinces in northern Italy and Gaul. He decided to campaign against the Celtic people and not only make Roman territory safer but increase it. Cicero, a famous orator, said of him in a speech to the senate:

"Before, members of the senate, we only had a route through Gaul. All the other territories were occupied by peoples who either were hostile to us or could not be trusted. Caesar has fought very successfully against the fiercest of peoples in great battles and made them part of the Roman state".

Civil war and after

Because of these successful military campaigns Julius Caesar became popular but aroused jealousy. When in 49 BC his rival Pompey persuaded the senate to order him to disband his army, civil war broke out. It ended four years later when Caesar defeated Pompey's sons in Spain. Caesar was now the most powerful person in Rome and declared himself "dictator for life".

Rome was no longer a republic, with people able to vote for their leaders. Marcus Brutus, Gaius Cassius and others plotted to kill Caesar and on March 15, 44 BC stabbed him to death outside the senate house.

△ A portrait of Julius Caesar in middle age carved in marble. The Roman writer Suetonius said that he was *"a bit of a dandy. He always had his hair carefully trimmed and used to comb his few hairs forward to cover his baldness."*

▽ Carthage in North Africa was completely destroyed by Rome in 146 BC, ending the war with the Carthaginian Empire. Caesar later made it a colony for retired soldiers.

Bronze helmet with horse hair crest

Pilum *or spear*

Mail shirt

Short sword

Oval shield

Hob-nailed leather sandals

◁ The most important public buildings in Rome were sited in the Forum Romanum. On the right are the ruins of the Basilica Julia – a great meeting hall built by Caesar.

▷ Coins often pictured great events in Roman history. Above is the coin minted in 48 BC to celebrate Caesar's victories in Gaul. The one below commemorates his murder, with the date, the "Ides of March".

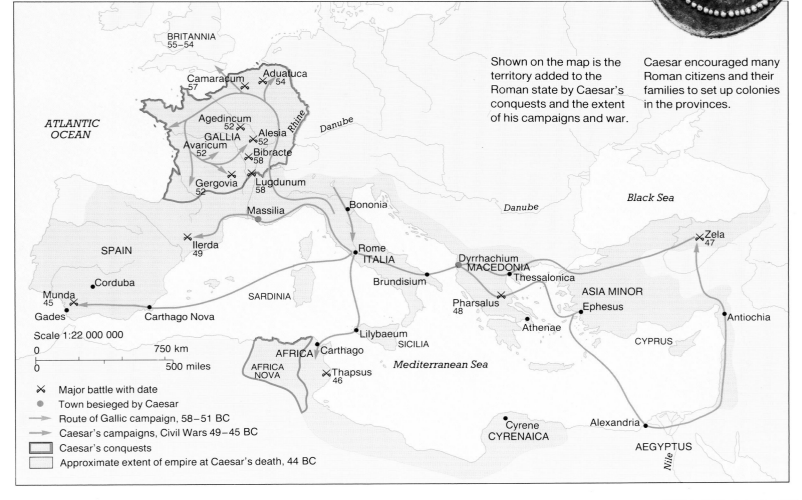

Shown on the map is the territory added to the Roman state by Caesar's conquests and the extent of his campaigns and war.

Caesar encouraged many Roman citizens and their families to set up colonies in the provinces.

BRITANNIA 55–54
Camaracum 57
Aduatuca 54
Agedincum 52
Alesia 52
GALLIA
Avaricum 52
Bibracte 58
Gergovia 52
Lugdunum 58
Rhine
Danube
ATLANTIC OCEAN
Massilia
Bononia
Danube
Black Sea
Ilerda 49
SPAIN
Rome ITALIA
Dyrrhachium MACEDONIA
Thessalonica
Zela 47
Corduba
Brundisium
Pharsalus 48
ASIA MINOR
Ephesus
Antiochia
Munda 45
Gades
Carthago Nova
SARDINIA
Athenae
CYPRUS
Scale 1:22 000 000
0 — 750 km
0 — 500 miles
Lilybaeum
SICILIA
Carthago
AFRICA
AFRICA NOVA
Thapsus 46
Mediterranean Sea
Cyrene CYRENAICA
Alexandria
AEGYPTUS
Nile

✕ Major battle with date
● Town besieged by Caesar
→ Route of Gallic campaign, 58–51 BC
→ Caesar's campaigns, Civil Wars 49–45 BC
▢ Caesar's conquests
▢ Approximate extent of empire at Caesar's death, 44 BC

◁ A full-time professional soldier. Julius Caesar could not have conquered so much new territory for the Roman state without such men.

▷ The forum of Caesar. The main building was a temple of Venus. A statue of the dictator on horse-back stood in the center of the square.

Caesar wins the civil war of 49-45 BC

49 BC Caesar marches on Rome. In Spain he destroys Pompey's army at Ilerda. Pompey flees to Greece.
48 BC At Dyrrhachium, Pompey breaks through Caesar's defences, but Caesar defeats him at the great battle of Pharsalus. Pompey is pursued to Egypt and is murdered before Caesar arrives.
47 BC Caesar establishes Cleopatra as queen in Egypt. He marches through Syria and Asia Minor to defeat Pompey's ally, Pharnaces of Pontus, at Zela.
46 BC Caesar adds Africa Nova to the Empire after defeating Pompey's two sons at Thapsus.
45 BC He defeats the Pompeian army at Munda.

ROMAN MEN AND WOMEN

A large amount of evidence survives to show us what Roman men and women looked like. The Romans liked sculpture, especially in stone. Stone statues and busts of emperors, gods and goddesses, and famous people were erected in the streets, public buildings and temples. Wealthy Romans had statues or busts of their ancestors in their homes.

We also find carved portraits on Roman tombstones and burial vaults. This tells us not only what people looked like but sometimes what they did. They might be pictured at work – a shoemaker, for example – or dressed in the clothes for their job – a soldier perhaps. Tombstones often give us other information about Roman people or their life. For instance, on a tombstone you might find a portrait of a woman with her family seated around a table, also her name and where she came from.

Portraits of emperors usually appear on Roman coins as well as on statues. Because rulers tend to want a bit of flattery in their official portraits, these may not always be a true likeness. The writer Suetonius said that the Emperor Claudius had "an uncontrollable laugh when angry, slobbered at the mouth and had a runny nose", but this does not show in any of his statues.

△ This bust shows a male hair-style and close-cropped beard typical of the period.

▷ This man has the distinctive Roman hooked nose, which Romans found attractive.

◁ The tombstone of a young man from Palmyra in Syria who died in the 2nd century AD. He wears a toga. The inscription is in his own language, Syriac.

▷ The work of the black-smith pictured on a burial monument. On the left an assistant or apprentice heats up the forge with bellows. He is protected from the heat by a large shield. The blacksmith (center) sits at the anvil hammering an object into shape. On the right are his tools – tongs and hammer – and below them a spear-head and a door-lock, two of his products.

▷ This lady from Pompeii wears gold ear-rings and what looks like a gold hair-net. She holds a "book" of wooden tablets, each covered with a thin layer of wax. Writing was done by marking the wax with the pointed stylus.

◁ A very elaborate hair-style worn by a lady (probably in the Emperor's court) of the 1st century AD.

▷ This toga-clad green-grocer set up his stall in the port of Ostia, where this sculpture was found on a burial monument. There is a basket for the goods under the trestle table, and on top the vegetables look like garlic, leeks and globe artichokes.

Hair-styles

Roman men and women of all classes were fussy about their hair and appearance. Up to the 2nd century AD most men were clean shaven, but after that beards became popular. Men's hair was sometimes cropped short but was usually combed slightly forward, as can be seen in these portraits.

Women's hair-styles could be fairly simple but also included very elaborate curls which must have occupied expert maids for a long time. Some women wore wigs or dyed their hair using extracts from plants, much as we do today.

Clothes

In some parts of the Roman world men wore tight trousers but in most places they wore a tunic like the blacksmith's shown below. Roman citizens (only men could be citizens) could wear the toga – a large semicircular piece of cloth wrapped loosely around the upper body. This was a symbol of manhood as well as citizenship. Women wore under-tunics with a dress called a *stola* on top. In the open air they might wear a *palla*, a loose-fitting garment.

Both men and women wore jewelry such as brooches, necklaces and rings.

POMPEII – STRUCK BY DISASTER

"Everything is drowned in the flames and buried in the ashes of sadness."

So wrote the Roman poet Martial about the destruction of the towns in the Bay of Naples by the volcano Vesuvius in AD 79. Pompeii and Herculaneum suffered the worst – so much so that they were never lived in again in the Roman period.

We know about the destruction because an eyewitness recorded the events. The writer Pliny was staying with his uncle, a commander of the Roman fleet stationed near by. He noted:

"On August 24 at about 1 p.m., my mother pointed out to Uncle an odd-shaped cloud. We could not make out which mountain it came from but later found out that it was from Vesuvius. The cloud was rising in a shape like a pine tree because it shot up to a great height in the form of a tall trunk, then spread out at the top into branches."

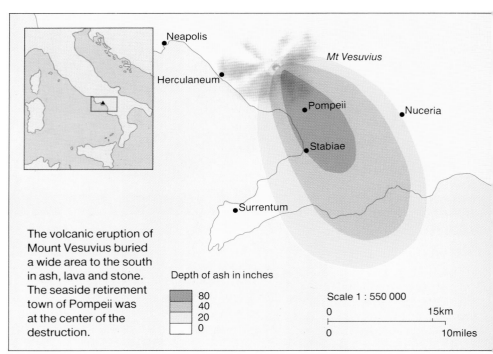

The volcanic eruption of Mount Vesuvius buried a wide area to the south in ash, lava and stone. The seaside retirement town of Pompeii was at the center of the destruction.

Depth of ash in inches

80
40
20
0

Scale 1 : 550 000

0   15km

0   10miles

The excavator Fiorelli would pour liquid plaster into the holes left by bodies enclosed in ash from Vesuvius. These people were probably overcome by fumes and must have suffocated to death. Casts sometimes show details of clothing and footwear, such as sandals.

△ Vesuvius deposited feet of ash and stone on top of Pompeii. A mud flow 66ft deep covered Herculaneum.

When the top of Vesuvius blew up, it rained down ash, stone and lava over a wide area. Some places such as Naples had just a thin coating of ash, but Pompeii was covered to a depth of nearly 13ft. About 2,000 people (from a population of 20,000) lost their lives – crushed, trapped in buildings or suffocated by the sulfur fumes. At Herculaneum the volcanic eruption caused a mud flow that completely covered all the buildings.

It took about three days for the sky to clear, and by then it was no longer possible to live in the towns. The Emperor Titus gave money for the relief of the refugees, but the towns were never rebuilt.

Rediscovery of a Roman town

Pompeii and Herculaneum were forgotten during the Roman period. They were not rediscovered until the 16th century. By the 18th century people had begun to excavate them.

A great deal of Pompeii, and some of Herculaneum, was dug up. These first excavations revealed parts of houses, shops, streets and public buildings. The work was very careless, though, and some of the remains were damaged. In 1860 the new director of excavations, Giuseppe Fiorelli, began to uncover large areas instead of digging holes everywhere. He carried out his work with care and often preserved whole buildings.

Town plan

Pompeii probably gives us the most detailed picture we have of a prosperous Roman town in the 1st century AD. It was originally an Etruscan town but was redeveloped several times. Much of the town was divided into regular blocks called *insulae* ("islands"). The town had a large forum (or market-place), two theaters, an amphitheater and several bathhouses enclosed by a stone wall.

◁ One of Pompeii's main streets leading to the forum, the town center. The roadway is paved, with wide walkways on either side. Most houses had a blank wall facing the street, to protect privacy, with just a simple doorway. Some of the buildings have been reconstructed.

▽ Stepping-stones helped people cross the dirty, wet streets. There were a number of shops opening straight on to the street.

THE EMPIRE OF AUGUSTUS

The Romans still talked about the Republic and voted for their officials, but the state had been in the hands of powerful men for many years. Politicians like Sulla, Pompey and Julius Caesar seized power, backed by their own troops.

Caesar had increased the size of the Roman Empire enormously. His murder caused another civil war. His adopted son and heir Octavian came back from Greece, where he was studying, to avenge his father's death.

The Empire divided

After several battles across the Empire the winners, Octavian and Marcus Antonius

(usually called Mark Antony now), divided the Roman world between them. Antony ruled the east from his base in Alexandria, Egypt, where he could be with his love Queen Cleopatra. Octavian ruled from Rome.

Neither Octavian nor the senate of Rome would allow the Roman state to remain split. War was declared against Cleopatra and Antony in 31 BC. Octavian won the war and declared peace for the Romans in 29 BC.

Mighty Augustus

Octavian was now all-powerful in the Roman state and in 27 BC was given the title Augustus ("a person to be respected") by the senate. In the same year, writes the geographer Strabo:

> *"Augustus divided the whole of his Empire into two parts, giving one portion to the Roman people and keeping the other portion to govern himself."*

Augustus also used the Roman legions to secure the Empire's frontiers in Spain and Germany. Some provinces now had governors appointed by the senate (senatorial provinces). The others (imperial provinces) had governors appointed by Augustus.

Governing the provinces

Augustus had chosen his provinces carefully. They were the ones where most of the armies were stationed. He also chose carefully the people to govern those provinces. He wanted governors who would be loyal to him.

Augustus kept Egypt as his own personal property and had a law passed forbidding any senator from entering the country without his personal permission.

The governor's staff

The governor's title in Latin was Legatus ("appointed person") Augusti ("by Augustus the Emperor") pro Praetore ("in his place as governor").

The governor was commander-in-chief and had 30 to 40 officials under him. An official called a procurator looked after the province's finances, and there were military staff, secretaries, messengers, couriers, personal assistants, lawyers and clerks.

▷ Part of the Altar of the Peace of Augustus, put up by the senate in Augustus' honor in 13 BC. The carving shows members of the imperial family taking part in annual sacrifices at the altar.

▽ The Roman Empire in 27 BC. In the provinces people's way of life became "Romanized". In 22 BC Augustus said that Narbonensis in Gaul was "more a part of Italy than a province". Legions of the Roman army were stationed throughout the Empire (few remained in Italy), and this helped the spread of Roman customs.

▽ This statue shows Augustus in a general's uniform at the age of about 45. The breastplate shows a defeated barbarian and a Roman officer.

ATLAN OCEA

TARRACONE

Douro

LUSITANIA

Tagus

BAETICA

Senatorial province
Imperial province
Scale 1:20 000 000

0

600 km

400 miles

Augustus, the first Emperor

March 15, 44 BC Julius Caesar murdered. Civil war breaks out.

31 BC Mark Antony and Cleopatra defeated by Octavian at the battle of Actium in Achaen.

January 11, 29 BC Octavian declares peace throughout the Roman world.

28 BC Octavian appointed Princeps Senatus ("leader of the senate"). He is now in control of the state's armies and its finances.

27 BC Octavian given the title Augustus. The eighth month, Sextilis, is now renamed Augustus.

23 BC Augustus takes complete control of all the provinces. After this he takes on more and more of the power of elected officials. The senate grants him extended powers.

15-13 BC Augustus lives in Gaul.

2 BC Augustus is granted the title Pater Patriae ("father of the country").

August 19, AD 14 Augustus dies at Nola.

September 17, AD 14 The senate decrees that the Emperor Augustus is one of the gods of Rome.

1 ALPES POENINAE
2 ALPES COTTIAE
3 ALPES MARITIMAE

TRAJAN'S ARMY

The Emperor Trajan built a breathtaking monument to the Roman army. He erected a huge column, covered with carvings, in the center of Rome. It was a record of his conquest of Dacia, north of the river Danube. The column's fine carvings show us what Roman soldiers and their enemies looked like, how they fought and how they built their camps. Trajan's wars made Dacia a new Roman province in AD 106.

Defending the frontiers

Once a new province was made part of the Roman Empire it had to be defended. Large armies were left to patrol the country. They had to build permanent forts to live in, with sturdy defensive walls. Hadrian's Wall was built along Britain's northern frontier, and similar walls along the rivers Rhine and Danube.

A fort was laid out in a very regular way with easy access to its walls and gates. The legionaries lived in barrack blocks built for units of about 80 to 100 men, with a centurion in charge. Other buildings inside the fort included the headquarters, hospital and stores.

The soldier's life

In the provinces a soldier had plenty of other work to do apart from fighting. In Egypt for example, besides training, detachments from the legions were sent out on guard duty at frontiers (to ensure that customs dues were paid), at mines and quarries, at road junctions and at grain supply depots. These examples are taken from the records of a legion in c. AD 80:

"Marcus Papirius Rufus – assigned to the granary in the Neapolis district of Alexandria as a secretary; Titus Saturnius – to harbor dredging; Titus Valens – to papyrus manufacture; Titus Celer – to the river patrol boat."

The Emperor Trajan did not always approve of soldiers doing "civilian" jobs. He wrote to the governor of Bithynia in AD 111:

"There is no need to withdraw any soldiers to guard the prisons. It is much better to observe our ancient custom of employing public slaves for this purpose – as few soldiers as possible should be taken off their normal duties."

▽ Trajan's column, put up after he conquered Dacia. Almost 100ft high, it had a statue of the Emperor Trajan on top – now replaced by St Peter.

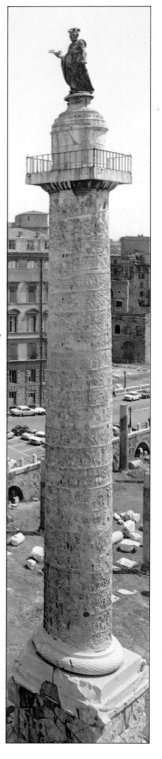

△ Soldiers shown building a fortified camp – a detail from Trajan's column. A soldier on the left keeps watch. The men's swords, helmets and shields are near by (far right). Some (right) dig out the defensive ditch and build a rampart, carrying the earth in baskets. Others strengthen the bank with wooden beams. The wall is made from squares of turf. Trajan stands inside the wall at the top, waiting for a Dacian prisoner (bottom left) to be brought up. The clothes of the two soldiers who are leading him by the hair show that they are auxiliary soldiers, recruited locally. To the left, more legionaries build a bridge over a stream, beyond which a sentry guards another camp.

◁ This artillery machine was called a *ballista*. Like a crossbow on a stand, it fired short, iron-tipped bolts with great accuracy.

▷ As protection against missiles, Roman soldiers would link shields together and make a roof of them so strong that other soldiers could walk over it. This was called *testudo* or "tortoise" formation.

▷ This drawing, taken from a scene on Trajan's column, shows the siege of Sarmizegethusa, the native capital of Dacia. Both legionary soldiers and auxiliaries are storming the walls of a Dacian strong-hold. Besides the *testudo*, *ballista* and *onager* (stone-hurling machine), the Romans used siege towers and huge iron-headed battering-rams mounted inside sheds on wheels.

PROVINCES AND FRONTIERS OF THE EMPIRE

Several emperors after Augustus added to the territory controlled by Rome. The Emperor Claudius himself took part in the invasion of Britain in AD 43 and he brought Thracia and Mauretania into the Empire. Trajan served in many parts of the Empire as a soldier and as provincial governor before becoming Emperor. He was later responsible for adding new territories, such as Dacia.

Guarding the new frontiers

By the 2nd century, when the Empire was at its largest, between 50 and 60 million people probably lived within its frontiers. There were only 30 legions and auxiliary troops to control this vast area – nearly 450,000 soldiers.

Some of these troops were stationed at frontiers, on Hadrian's Wall in Britain, for example. The Emperor Hadrian, builder of that wall, traveled widely. He was interested in the provinces and wanted to make sure his frontiers were safe.

Roads and communications

The Roman Empire needed efficient communications – especially roads that could be used all year round, even in wet winter weather. Troops had to be able to move quickly to trouble spots; messages needed to be passed back to camps and to Rome.

Good roads and harbors were also necessary so that goods could be transported into and around the Empire.

Imperial couriers

Augustus established an official courier service, the *cursus publicus*, to carry mail and people traveling on public business. It was expensive to maintain relays of horses and carriages on all the major routes through the Empire. This was paid for, at least at first, by the cities and towns the roads passed through.

▷ Provinces and frontiers of the Empire to 106 AD.

New provinces gained by Rome

3rd century BC: 241 BC Sicilia. **238 BC** Sardinia. **227 BC** Corsica.

2nd century BC: 146 BC Greece and Africa. **133-129 BC** Asia. **121 BC** Gallia Narbonensis. **101 BC** Cilicia.

1st century BC: 74 BC Cyrenaica. **68-67 BC** Creta. **64-63 BC** Syria, Bithynia and Pontus. **58 BC** Cyprus. **58-52 BC** Gallia. **30 BC** Aegyptus. **27 BC** Spanish provinces. **25 BC** Galatia. **15 BC** Alpes Poeninae. **14 BC** Alpes Maritimae. **16-9 BC** Raetia, Noricum, Pannonia and Dalmatia.

1st and 2nd centuries AD: AD 6 Judaea. **AD 17** Cappadocia. **AD 40** Mauretania. **AD 43** Britannia, Lycia and Pamphylia. **AD 46** Thracia. **AD 58** Alpes Cottiae. **AD 85-6** Moesia divided into two provinces. **AD 90** Germania. **AD 106** Arabia and Dacia.

ATLANTIC OCEAN

LUSITANIA
Emerita Augusta

Corduba
BAETICA

Tingi

MAURETANIA TINGITANA

Roman acquisitions by
201 BC
100 BC
44 BC
AD14
AD96
AD106

△ Horse-drawn stage-coach with passengers riding on top as well as inside. Journeys were slow, bumpy and dirty.

▷ Roman roads are often (but not always) straight. This one is called the Fosse Way, in Somerset, England.

On the road
Travelling officials were able to use the government rest-houses, *mansiones*. Others made do with road-

Travelers

Eburacum

BRITANNIA

Londinium

GERMANIA
INFERIOR
Colonia Agrippina

BELGICA
Durocorotorum
Moguntiacum

LUGDUNENSIS

Augusta Vindelicorum

AQUITANIA
Lugdunum
GERMANIA
SUPERIOR
RAETIA
NORICUM
Carnuntum

Virunum
Aquincum

...gala
Axima
PANNONIA

NARBONENSIS
Segusio
DACIA
Sarmizegetusa

Narbo
2 3
Viminacium

...RACONENSIS
Cemenelum
DALMATIA
Salonae
MOESIA
SUPERIOR
MOESIA INFERIOR

Black Sea

CORSICA
ITALIA
THRACIA
Amastris
BITHYNIA AND
PONTUS

Tarraco
Aleria
Rome
Perinthus
Nicomedia

SARDINIA
MACEDONIA
Thessalonica
Ancyra
CAPPADOCIA

Carales
ASIA
Caesarea

...AURETANIA
...ESARIENSIS
Caesarea
Carthago
SICILIA
EPIRUS
ACHAEA
Ephesus
GALATIA
Tarsus

AFRICA
Syracusae
Corinthus
LYCIA
AND
PAMPHYLIA
CILICIA
Antiochia
SYRIA

Gortyn
CYPRUS
Paphos

CRETA
Caesarea
Bostra

Mediterranean Sea
JUDAEA

Province capital, where known
ALPES POENINAE
...LPES COTTIAE
...LPES MARITIMAE

Cyrene
Alexandria
ARABIA

...e 1:20 000 000

600 km
400 miles

CYRENAICA
AEGYPTUS

side inns. People who were rich enough might travel in a litter, called a *lectica*, carried by four strong bearers. Journeys were slow, by modern standards. Strong walkers could cover about 20 to 25mi in a day. Others traveled on horseback or by coach. The imperial post would shoot past, covering over 40mi each day. The poet Horace commented about one journey: "We arrived quite worn out. It was to be expected. The journey was long, and the road conditions were awful because of heavy rain."

Supplies   Pedestrians and salesmen   Wine tanker   Despatch riders

MEN OF POWER: THE EMPERORS

When the rules, or constitution, of Roman government were first worked out, there was no word for "emperor". The Romans had always hated the word *rex* ("king"), which offended their idea of democracy. They wanted republican rule, which meant rule through elected officials.

Last of the dictators

In times of crisis, however, the Romans would appoint a *dictator*. This was someone, usually a former consul, legally appointed to take full control of the government for a limited time. Julius Caesar was appointed dictator in 46 BC.

When civil war ended in 31 BC, it was clear that the vast Roman world could no longer be ruled by Roman democracy. Too many ambitious men, such as Caesar, had taken power for themselves with the backing of the army.

First of the emperors

The winner of the civil war was Augustus, grandson of Caesar's sister and his adopted son. He became the first Emperor and established 30 years of peace.

From Augustus' time onwards, formal titles were given to the Emperor. The name Augustus, meaning "someone who is respected", was given to him in 27 BC. He also took his adopted father's name, Caesar. Both

▽ This coin pictures the joint Emperors Diocletian and Maximian.

▷ Roman emperors, from Augustus to Justinian – and the end of the Empire.

27 BC-AD 14	Augustus
14-37	Tiberius
37-41	Gaius Caligula
41-54	Claudius
54-68	Nero

68-69	Galba
69	Otho, Vitellius

69-79	Vespasian
79-81	Titus
81-96	Domitian
96-98	Nerva
97-117	Trajan (97-98 with Nerva)
117-38	Hadrian
138-61	Antoninus Pius
161-80	Marcus Aurelius (161-169 with Lucius Verus)
180-92	Commodus

193	Pertinax
193	Didius Julianus
193-211	Septimius Severus
211-17	Caracalla (211-212 with Geta)
217-18	Macrinus
218-22	Elagabalus
222-35	Alexander Severus

Time of disorder in the Empire (235-284)

235-38	Maximinus
238	Gordian I and II (in Africa)
238	Balbinus and Pupienus (in Italy)
238-44	Gordian III
244-49	Philip
249-51	Decius
251-53	Trebonianus Gallus
253	Aemilianus
253-60	Valerian
253-68	Gallienus (253-260 with Valerian)

WEST		EAST	
259-74	Gallic empire of Postumus, Victorinus, Tetricus	260-72	Palmyrene empire of Odaenathus, Zenobia, Vaballath
268-70	Claudius		
270	Quintillus		
270-75	Aurelian		
275-76	Tacitus		
276-82	Probus		
282-83	Carus		
283-84	Carinus and Numerian		

284-305 Diocletian and Tetrarchy

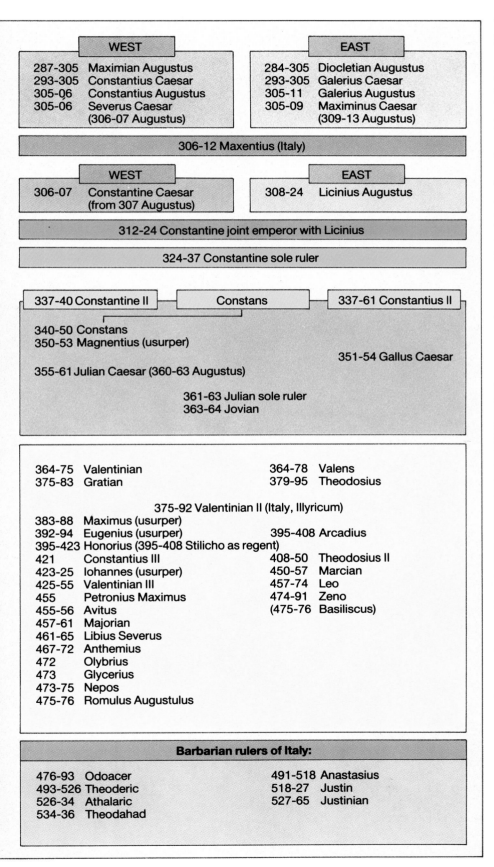

"Augustus" and "Caesar" became titles meaning Emperor.

The Latin word *imperator*, originally a title given to a successful military commander, was also now used. Emperors had other formal titles which appeared on coins, inscriptions and public announcements, such as Pater Patriae ("Father of the Country") and Princeps ("First Citizen").

The good, the bad and the mad

Some emperors ruled well and developed the Roman state. Hadrian, for example, journeyed around the Empire, organizing large-scale rebuilding in each province.

Other Emperors were cruel and murdered their rivals and opponents or wasted public money. Some, according to Roman writers, were dangerously mad. The Emperor Gaius Caligula was said to have planned to make his favorite horse a consul.

△ This mosaic picture is of the Emperor Justinian. He reconquered much of the western Empire which had been taken over by the Vandals in Africa, the Ostrogoths in Italy and the Visigoths in Spain. The lands were gradually lost again.

GODS AND SPIRITS: ROMAN RELIGION

The early Romans believed that gods, goddesses and powerful spirits were everywhere and controlled human actions. Gods and spirits might be friendly if offerings and prayers were made to them. This could happen in temples, at roadside or household altars or at other sacred places. The offerings included honey cakes, fruit and wine poured out on the ground. Often animals were sacrificed.

Gods and goddesses

As time went on, the Romans adopted gods and goddesses from other peoples, especially the Etruscans and the Greeks. They thought of these beings as large-size humans and portrayed them in statues and paintings. Some gods were more important than others, but each had a special responsibility.

The "king and queen" of the Roman deities were Jupiter (great god of the sky) and Juno (patron goddess of women). Others included: Minerva (wisdom, crafts and industries), Venus (beauty and love), Mars (war), Vulcan (fire), Vesta (hearth and home), Mercury (merchants) and Janus (two-headed god of doorways). Many other gods and goddesses were worshiped throughout the Roman Empire.

Emperor worship

When Rome became an empire, emperors were considered to be gods too, and temples were built for their worship. Several emperors were worshiped as gods before they died.

▷ Worship of the god Mithras was brought to Rome in the 1st century AD. Here Mithras is shown killing a bull, whose flowing blood was thought to be a source of life.

▷ Underground temple to Mithras in Rome. Mithraism was carried by soldiers and merchants all over the Empire. It was a "men only" religion.

▽ Circular temple in Rome dedicated to the god Hercules who was said to have performed one of his 12 labors here. It was built in the 2nd century BC in the Greek style.

◁ A 4th-century AD mosaic floor from a villa in Dorset, Britain. The center-piece shows the head of Christ and the first two letters of his name in Greek: x (Ch) and r (r).

Ceremonies and temples

Worship of a god or goddess usually involved processions, sacrifices and offerings at an altar. The *pontifex* or priest carried out the ceremony for the people.

Fine temples were built in the center of towns and cities for the important god and the ones considered special by the townspeople. The Emperor Hadrian completed a large temple which you can still see in Rome called the Pantheon, dedicated to all the gods. This has a dome 148ft in both height and diameter, which is the largest ever built by pre-industrial methods. The inside of the dome was meant to represent the heavens, and the opening at the top symbolized the sun.

People also built altars inside their houses at which they could make offerings to the gods who protected the household.

Foreign religions

The Romans also accepted into their religion gods and goddesses who were worshiped in countries they ruled. In Egypt they came across Isis and Serapis, in Persia there was Mithras and in Britain the sun-goddess Sul.

Some religions, however, were outlawed by the Romans. Roman armies fought several wars against the Jews and hunted down the Druids, the priests of the Celtic peoples of Gaul and Britain. At first Christians were persecuted, but finally Christianity became the official state religion in AD 312.

◁ This sculpture from the arch of Titus in Rome shows the destruction of the Jewish Temple in Jerusalem in AD 70, when the gold seven-branched candlestick (the menorah) was carried off.

▽ Every five years the Romans held a census. This began with a ceremony at which a bull, a ram and a pig were killed as a sacrifice to the gods.

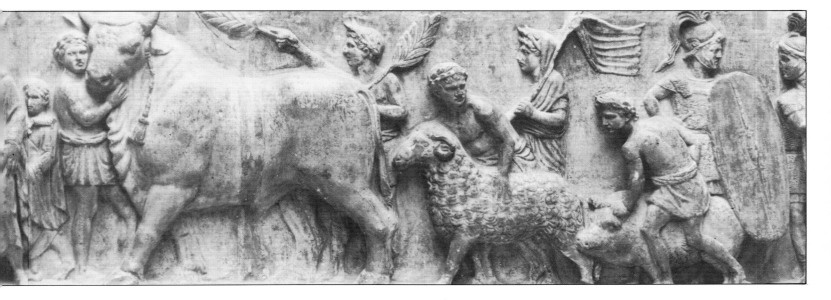

THE ROMAN BATHS

At least one bath-house was considered essential for any Roman town. Pompeii had three big baths which the public could use, and everyone used them. It was cheap to get in, and children had free entrance. The baths were important places for relaxing, seeing friends or even holding business meetings.

From cold dip to sauna

Some baths, such as the Stabian Baths at Pompeii, had separate facilities for men and women. If not, there were special times set aside for each group. First you undressed (in the *apodyterium*) and left your clothes in a locker or on a shelf. From there you passed into the cold, unheated room called a *frigidarium* and had a cold dip. Next you went into a warm room, the *tepidarium*.

From there you passed into the *caldarium*, the really hot room full of steam, with hot dip baths and a warm fountain for washing. This was heated by means of a hypocaust – a hollow space under the floor into which hot air was blown. The steam sweated out the dirt, which could be scraped off. A slave might do this for you and then massage you and oil your skin. There was also a *laconicum* or sauna to go through if you wanted intense dry heat.

▷ The Stabian Baths at Pompeii. Men's baths: **1** dressing-room, **2** cold room, **3** warm room, **4** hot room, **5** sauna. Women's baths: **6** dressing-room, **7** warm room, **8** hot room. **9** Furnaces. **10** Exercise yard. **11** Swimming-pool. **12** Lavatories.

Ear-scoop

Strigils and flask

Nail-file

(not to scale)

◁ Instruments used at the baths. The curved bronze *strigils* were for scraping off the sweat and dirt. The flasks had a mixture of olive oil and pumice for cleaning and refreshing the skin.

Afterwards you could go out into the open courtyard for exercise – perhaps a ball game or just a walk. There was also a small swimming-pool and lavatories.

Working in the baths

Large numbers of slaves were needed to keep the baths going. The heat for the rooms and the water was produced in a furnace which blew hot air under the floors and up through the walls to the roof. Floors above hypocausts were raised on pillars. Other slaves carried out massage or brought towels. Food sellers would come in with trays of snacks or sweets.

Noisy place to live

"I live over the public baths – you know what that means. Ugh! It's sickening. First there are the 'strongmen' doing their exercises and swinging heavy lead weights about with grunts and groans. Next the lazy ones having a cheap massage – I can hear someone being slapped on the shoulders. Then there's the man who always likes the sound of his own voice in the bath. And what about the ones who leap into the pool making a huge splash!" – Lucius Seneca, in Rome about AD 63.

▽ The Great Bath at Bath, in England. The Romans valued the pure spring water here for its excellent health-giving properties.

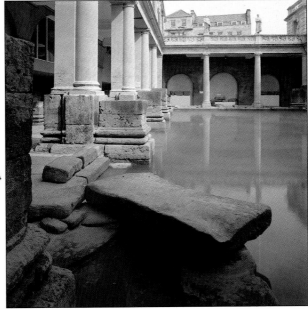

IMPERIAL ROME

"I found Rome built of sun-dried bricks. I leave a city covered in marble." This is what the Emperor Augustus is said to have boasted at the end of his reign. The city of Rome, now with a population of over a million, needed complete reorganization. Augustus was the first to carry out large-scale redevelopment and he did indeed transform the city.

Two great fires

During the reign of the Emperor Nero a serious fire swept through Rome. The historian Tacitus tells us that in this disaster of AD 64 only 4 of Rome's 14 districts survived. Some were completely destroyed right down to ground level; in others only a few houses survived.

Nero began to rebuild the city to include an enormous palace for himself. We are told by the writer Suetonius that the Golden House, as it was called, stood in a great park, and parts of the building were covered in gold. When it was finished, Nero – a vain and foolish man – is reported to have said: "Good, now I can live like a human being at last!"

Nero's Golden House was destroyed by another fire in AD 104. Only his colossal statue

▽ This arch, built in AD 203, commemorates the triumphs of the Emperor Septimius Severus and his sons over the Parthians and Arabs.

Imperial Rome was a large city, but most of its people were poor. Their living accommodation – blocks of apartments – was poorly built and has vanished without a trace. Only the better-constructed public buildings have survived. These include temples, baths, theaters and arches, as well as much of the city wall and several bridges across the river Tiber.

Hills of Rome

N

Aqua Virgo

Temple of Fortuna

Ara Pacis Augustae

SERVIAN WALL

0   500 meters
0   1500 feet

Mausoleum of Augustus
Temple of the Sun of Aurelius

Baths of Diocletian

Mausoleum of Hadrian

Solar clock of Augustus

Tiber

Temple of the Divine Hadrian

Aelian Bridge

Baths of Nero

Bridge of Nero

Arch of Claudius

Stadium of Domitian (Piazza Navona)

Temple of Serapis

Temple of Isis

Odeion of Domitian

Temple of Juno Lucina

Baths of Agrippa

Portico of

Porticus Minuc a Frumentaria

see inset

Baths of Trajan

Theater and crypt of Balbus

Baths of Titus

Bridge of Agrippa

Portico of Octavia

Site of House

Bridge of Aurelius

Theater of Marcellus

Temple of Venus and Rome

Ludus Magnus

Mithrae

Palace of Tiberius

Colosseum

Aqua Alsietina

Temple of Apollo

Temple of Elagabalus

Temple of the Divine Claudius

Temple of Ceres, Liber and Libera

Palace of Domitian

Circus Maximus

Palace of Septimius Severus

Temple of Luna

Septizodium

Temple of Minerva

Temple of Diana

Baths of Licinius Sura

Temple of Bona Dea

Baths of Decius

Tiber

Porticus Aemilia

Baths of Caracalla

Horrea Galbana

Horrea Lolliana

▷ Rome's main forum. Many emperors added temples, statues and arches. Overlooking the forum is Trajan's market, a multi-story group of buildings set into the hill-side. Here there were shops and business premises. The forum was the Empire's center of government, religion and business.

**Map labels:**
QUIRINAL · SUBURANA · Market of Trajan · Temple of Mars Ultor · Temple of Pax · Library · Basilica Ulpia · Forum of Augustus · Forum of Trajan · Forum of Nerva · Forum of Julius Caesar · Curia · Temple of Trajan · Clivus Argentarius · Comitium · Tabularium · Sacra Via · Vicus Tuscus · Nova Via · Vicus Iugarius · N · CAPITOL

1. Column of Trajan
2. Libraries
3. Atrium Libertatis
4. Equestrian statue of Trajan
5. Temple of Venus Genetrix
6. Temple of Antoninus and Faustina
7. Regia
8. Temple of Julius Caesar
9. Arch of Augustus
10. Temple of Vesta
11. Atrium Vestae
12. Temple of Castor
13. Argiletum
14. Temple of Saturn
15. Rostra
16. Arch of Septimius Severus
17. Portico of the Di Consentes
18. Temple of Vespasian
19. Temple of Concord
20. Forum Romanum
21. Temple of Minerva
22. Temple of Juno Moneta

amp the aetorians

AURELIAN WALL

Nympheum (Temple of Minerva Medica)

Aqua Claudia

Temple of Saturn

Aqua Claudia

Colosseum

Temple of Juno Moneta

which stood in the entrance hall, survived, giving its name to the amphitheater which was later built close by: the Colosseum. On part of the site of Nero's palace, the Emperor Trajan built his baths.

Aqueducts and baths

It was not only Augustus and Nero who carried out grand building schemes. In AD 52 the Emperor Claudius completed a huge aqueduct which had been started by Caligula. This aqueduct, called Aqua Claudia, brought water to Rome from a source 40mi away.

Large amounts of water were needed for the huge baths which several emperors had built. The three largest groups of baths were those of Trajan, Caracalla and Diocletian.

Forum and temples

The greatest changes since republican times were probably in the city center around the main forum. The forum, or open square, was where the business of the city was carried out. Around it, buildings called basilicas were used for meetings, law courts and business.

In Imperial Rome, the forum became so important for ceremonies and religion that it was no longer used as a market-place. Other markets were built for particular goods, such as the *forum boarium* (cattle market) near the Circus Maximus.

Many temples were built. The temple of Saturn stood on the edge of the forum. The temple of Venus and Roma was built in AD 135 near Nero's ruined palace.

The temple of Juno Moneta towered above, on a nearby hill. "Moneta" (from the Latin *monere*, to warn) meant that Juno warned the Romans of an enemy approaching. The temple later became a place for minting coins. Our word "money" comes from this Latin word.

On the outskirts of town

Despite its magnificent public buildings, the poor people of Rome lived in appalling slums. By the 3rd century AD the city had expanded so much that a new wall was needed to encircle and defend it. For the first time in Rome's history this new Aurelian Wall went around the camp of the army unit which provided the Emperor with his defense.

ARENA AND STADIUM

All over the Empire, Romans enjoyed plays and concerts at the theater, chariot racing at the stadium and bloody sports at the amphitheater. Going to the amphitheater was probably the most popular. These oval-shaped buildings could hold huge crowds, often the entire population of a town. People would spend the whole day there.

Gladiators in combat

Various kinds of combat were staged in the amphitheatre. Most popular were the bouts between fighters, called gladiators, who struggled with each other to the death. Rich people and politicians paid for schools of gladiators to arrange the bouts. The gladiators were armed in different ways to make the fights more interesting. There were gladiators completely covered with armor, others fighting with just a sword and shield and some, called *retiarii*, who fought with a net and three-pronged spear.

Gladiators were usually slaves or war captives. Those who fought well and entertained the crowd might be given their freedom. At lunchtime there was usually a chance to see convicted criminals fight to the death. The last one left alive was brought back to fight again the next day.

Man against beast

Wild animals – such as lions, bears, snakes, deer and even elephants – would be fought by gladiators in the arena. Huge numbers were imported from the provinces, especially after some species had become extinct in Italy.

Amphitheaters were sometimes flooded for sea battles, complete with crocodiles to eat those who fell overboard. Not all Romans were entertained by combat and death. In the 1st century BC Marcus Cicero wrote:

"What pleasure can it give a person of taste when either a feeble human being is torn to pieces by an incredibly strong wild animal or a handsome beast is transfixed by a spear?"

Chariot racing

An exciting and dangerous sport enjoyed by many thousands was chariot racing. Many towns had a stadium where four teams – wearing red, blue, green and white colors – raced round a central barrier.

In the biggest stadium of all, the Circus Maximus in Rome, those charioteers who survived the race had traveled about 4mi during their seven laps of the large stadium. Some charioteers became idols of the crowd and earned huge sums of money.

△ This model of ancient Rome shows the Circus Maximus and the Colosseum (top right).

◁ This ampitheater at El Djem in North Africa was the third largest in the Empire.

▷ The games were public shows that involved danger and excitement, as in chariot races, far right. Gladiatorial combats resulted in blood-letting, in front of as many as 50,000 people.

For much of the 3rd century AD there was unrest in the Roman Empire. There were raids along all the frontiers. Forts had to be built on the coasts of Britain and northern Gaul. Between AD 235 and 284 there were more than 18 emperors, lasting only a few years before they were murdered or expelled.

The legions elect Diocletian

One of the most important changes in the history of the Roman Empire happened in AD 284. Diocletian, born in the province of Dalmatia, was the commander of Emperor Numerian's bodyguard. When Numerian was murdered, the army chose Diocletian to succeed him as Emperor.

Reorganization of Empire and army

Diocletian's main reform was to divide the huge Empire into two. He ruled the east from Nicomedia in Bithynia. He chose an old friend, Maximian, to be Emperor in the west, ruling from Rome. In AD 293 he established "four-man" rule by appointing two successors to help each Emperor. The arrangement worked, and Diocletian did not need to visit Rome until ten years later.

The Empire was reorganized into 12 districts called dioceses. Each had a governor called a *vicarius*. The army was enlarged at this time. The legions were also reorganized into permanent frontier troops and small mobile units which could be moved quickly wherever they were needed.

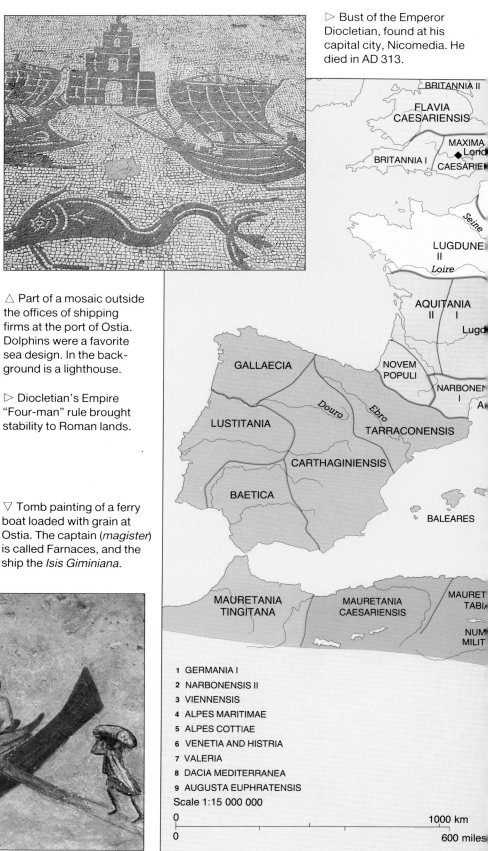

▷ Bust of the Emperor Diocletian, found at his capital city, Nicomedia. He died in AD 313.

△ Part of a mosaic outside the offices of shipping firms at the port of Ostia. Dolphins were a favorite sea design. In the background is a lighthouse.

▷ Diocletian's Empire "Four-man" rule brought stability to Roman lands.

1 GERMANIA I
2 NARBONENSIS II
3 VIENNENSIS
4 ALPES MARITIMAE
5 ALPES COTTIAE
6 VENETIA AND HISTRIA
7 VALERIA
8 DACIA MEDITERRANEA
9 AUGUSTA EUPHRATENSIS

Scale 1:15 000 000

0 ————————— 1000 km
0 ————————— 600 miles

▽ Tomb painting of a ferry boat loaded with grain at Ostia. The captain (*magister*) is called Farnaces, and the ship the *Isis Giminiana*.

The reforms of Diocletian

AD 211 The Emperor Septimius Severus dies in York. There are now about 46 provinces in the Empire, but many are later subdivided.

AD 284 Diocletian declared Emperor.

AD 286 Maximian made Emperor in the west.

AD 293 Diocletian creates a "rule of four men": two Emperors rule alongside two successors.

AD 296 Diocletian reorganizes the Empire's finances. Prices are fixed for coins of gold, silver and bronze. From now on all minting is done by the state. New tax system introduced.

AD 301 Diocletian issues official list of prices for goods throughout the Empire. But the system is abandoned as unworkable.

AD 303 In ill health Diocletian gives up the throne.

AD 313 Diocletian dies.

AD 314 The Empire now has 101 provinces.

AD 330 The Emperor Constantine the Great moves the capital of a reunited Roman Empire to Constantinople.

Diocletian dioceses

- Hispaniae
- Viennensis
- Galliae
- Britanniae
- Italia
- Pannoniae
- Moesiae
- Thraciae
- Asiana
- Pontica
- Oriens
- Africa

— Severan province boundary

— Diocletian province boundary

CARIA Diocletian province name

♦ Principal Roman mint

RMANIA II

Treveri
GICA II

EQUANIA

1

Rhine

Danube

II

RAETIA I

NORICUM RIPENSE

NORICUM MEDITERRANEUM

PANNONIA I

ALPES GRAIAE

6

7

AEMILIA

Aquileia

Mediolanum

Ticinum

LIGURIA

4 5

Po

Ravenna
FLAMINIA

Siscia
SAVIA

Sirmium
PANNONIA II

SCYTHIA

Danube

Black Sea

TUSCIA AND UMBRIA

PICENUM

Tiber

DALMATIA

MOESIA I

DACIA

Serdica

8

MOESIA II

PONTUS

PONTUS POLEMONIACUS

RSICA

SAMNIUM
Rome

PRAEVALITANA

DARDANIA

THRACIA

HAEMIMONTUS

DIOSPONTUS

PAPHLAGONIA

APULIA AND CALABRIA

MACEDONIA

RHODOPE

Heraclea

Constantinopolis

Nicomedia

EUROPA

ARMENIA MINOR

CAMPANIA

EPIRUS NOVA

Thessalonica

Cuzicus
HELLESPONTUS

BITHYNIA

GALATIA

Kizil Irmak

CAPPADOCIA

SARDINIA

LUCANIA AND BRUTTII

THESSALIA

LYDIA

PHRYGIA I II

PISIDIA

9

MESOPOTAMIA

EPIRUS VETUS

ASIA

CARIA

CILICIA

OSRHOENE

ACHAEA

INSULAE

LYCIA AND PAMPHYLIA

ISAURIA

Antiochia
SYRIA COELE

Carthago

PROCONSULARIS

MIDIA TENSIS

SICILIA

Catania

CRETA

CYPRUS

PHOENICIA

AUGUSTA LIBANENSIS

BYZACENA

Mediterranean Sea

PALAESTINA

ARABIA I

TRIPOLITANIA

LIBYA SUPERIOR

LIBYA INFERIOR

Alexandria

AEGYPTUS IOVIA

ARABIA II

AEGYPTUS HERCULIA

Nile

Red Sea

THEBAIS

THE ROMAN SHIP

Everyone living in the Roman world relied on food and other goods carried to them by ship. Large quantities of food, such as wheat, could be transported much more easily by ship than across land. By the 2nd century AD routes had been established all over the Roman Empire.

Luxury goods came to Rome and other towns from as far away as India and China.

"The arrival and departure of ships never stops – it is amazing that the sea, not to mention the harbor, is big enough for these merchant ships." – Aelius Aristides

Ostia – the port of Rome

Rome, capital of the Empire, needed a harbor by the sea. The Emperor Claudius constructed an artificial harbor near the port of Ostia at the Tiber's mouth to cope with the enormous volume of trade. In AD 103, 50 years later, the Emperor Trajan made this harbor even bigger and connected it to Ostia by a deep channel.

In the 2nd century AD about 50,000 people lived and worked in Ostia. Private firms carried out most of the trade in the port and built great warehouses, as well as smart offices in the center of the town.

△ A ship is about to dock. This scene, carved in marble in about AD 200, was found near Trajan's harbor. The flaming lighthouse seen behind the ship is probably the one recorded as built by the Emperor Claudius.

▽ This merchant ship could have carried about 6,000 amphorae. The oars at the back are for steering the ship. The large wooden goose's head represents the Egyptian goddess Isis, the seafarer's guardian.

▽ A ship unloading its cargo of wine, oil, wheat and cloth at Ostia. Much of the wheat would be used as free dole for the 200,000 people of Rome who were unemployed or very poor.

△ Roman warships were built for speed. About 300 oarsmen sweated to drive a ship forward. A ram at the ship's prow could hole an enemy ship underwater. A warship also carried 120 marines who could rush an enemy ship across ramps.

▷ Amphorae, great pottery flasks, were used to hold wine, fruit, olive-oil and the fish sauce much used in Roman cooking. When Trajan built his harbor at Ostia most of the wine and fish sauce came from Gaul.

PART TWO

THE GEOGRAPHY OF AN EMPIRE

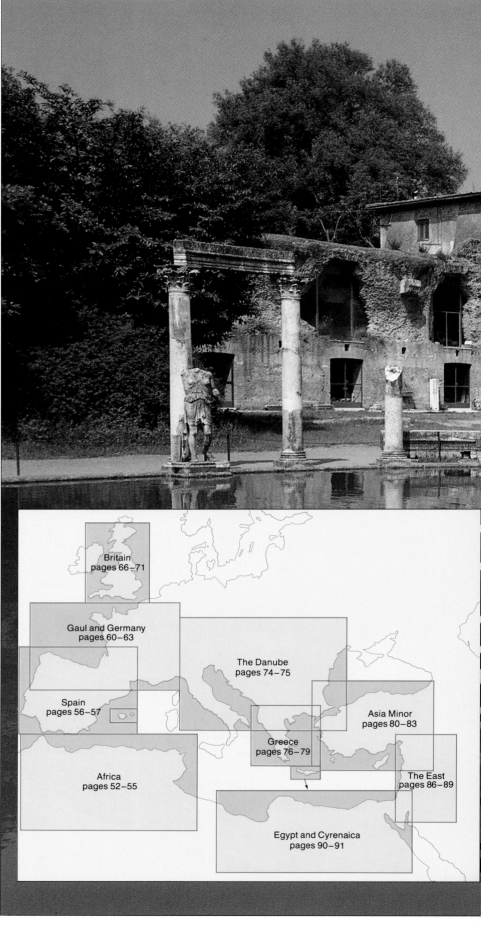

Britain
pages 66–71

Gaul and Germany
pages 60–63

The Danube
pages 74–75

Spain
pages 56–57

Asia Minor
pages 80–83

Greece
pages 76–79

Africa
pages 52–55

The East
pages 86–89

Egypt and Cyrenaica
pages 90–91

△ A wealthy Roman woman, about 50 BC.

▷ Hadrian's villa near Rome, AD 125-135.
Inset: Key to maps in this section of the book.

AFRICA

The Romans began to rule the province of Africa in 146 BC, after the destruction of Carthage. At first the province consisted of the land we now know as Tunisia. Later Roman territory stretched as far as Libya to the east and Morocco to the west. Mountains and deserts formed its southern borders.

Exporting to the Empire

This was a very rich part of the Roman world. At one time it supplied two-thirds of Rome's corn supply. The province's olives and olive-oil were exported to other parts of the Roman Empire. Archaeologists have found olive presses and great storage jars sunk into the ground in many African villas.

Africa also supplied wild animals for the amphitheaters of the Empire. North African leopards, wild asses, rhinos, lions, elephants, antelopes, zebra, giraffes and ostriches were "hunted" and killed as part of the public games in many Roman cities.

◁ The water source for Carthage was more than 30mi away, and so an aqueduct had to be built to carry the water. Water was stored in huge cisterns in the city.

▷ This colorful mosaic decorated a town house in Thugga (now called Dougga). The man is fishing with much the same equipment as we use today: rod, landing net and even a basket for the catch.

It was the Roman army which was responsible for making Africa a prosperous part of the Empire. About 28,000 troops patrolled this region from their network of forts and camps. Soldiers built roads and surveyed the countryside. The land was divided into regular plots, and great farming estates were created. Many of these estates were owned by the Emperor or by wealthy people living in far-off Rome.

New colonies

There had been a number of towns on the North African coast before the Romans arrived. Carthage had been Hannibal's capital city. In the west, in Mauretania, the Emperor Augustus established 12 new colonies for retired soldiers and their families.

These new townspeople soon helped build a Roman way of life on the southern shores of the Mediterranean. But the people who originally lived there still kept their language and some of their own way of life.

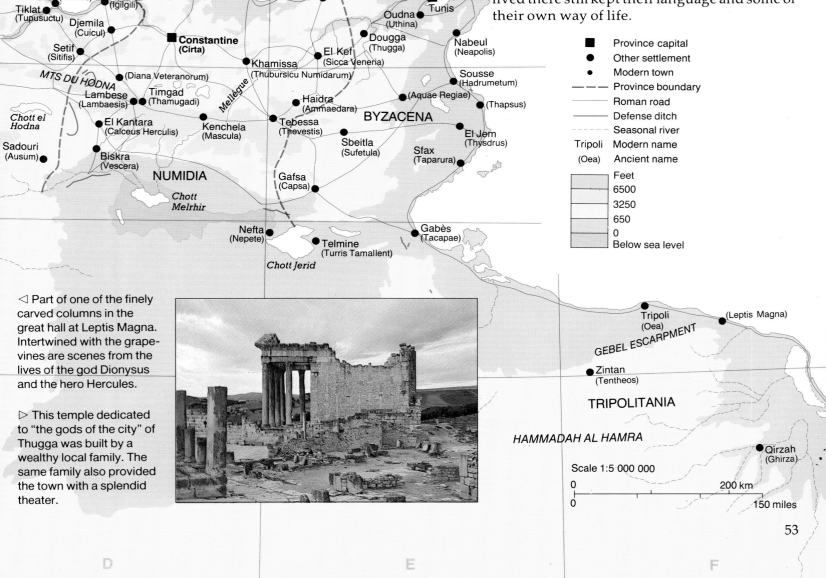

■	Province capital
●	Other settlement
•	Modern town
– – –	Province boundary
——	Roman road
——	Defense ditch
- - -	Seasonal river
Tripoli	Modern name
(Oea)	Ancient name

	Feet
	6500
	3250
	650
	0
	Below sea level

ucurru)
Bejaia (Saldae)
Jijel (Igilgili)
Tiklat (Tupusuctu)
Djemila (Cuicul)
Setif (Sitifis)
MTS DU HODNA
Lambese (Lambaesis)
Timgad (Thamugadi)
Chott el Hodna
El Kantara (Calceus Herculis)
Kenchela (Mascula)
Sadouri (Ausum)
Biskra (Vescera)
NUMIDIA
Chott Melrhir
Annaba (Hippo Regius)
Tabarka (Thabraca)
Constantine (Cirta)
Khamissa (Thubursicu Numidarum)
(Diana Veteranorum)
Mellègue
Haidra (Ammaedara)
Tebessa (Thevestis)
Gafsa (Capsa)
Nefta (Nepete)
Telmine (Turris Tamallent)
Chott Jerid
Bizerte (Hippo Diarrhytus)
AFRICA PROCONSULARIS
Utique (Utica)
■ (Carthago)
Tunis
Oudna (Uthina)
Dougga (Thugga)
El Kef (Sicca Veneria)
Nabeul (Neapolis)
Sousse (Hadrumetum)
(Aquae Regiae)
(Thapsus)
BYZACENA
Sbeitla (Sufetula)
El Jem (Thysdrus)
Sfax (Taparura)
Gabès (Tacapae)
Tripoli (Oea)
GEBEL ESCARPMENT
(Leptis Magna)
Zintan (Tentheos)
TRIPOLITANIA
HAMMADAH AL HAMRA
Qirzah (Ghirza)

Scale 1:5 000 000

0 — 200 km
0 — 150 miles

◁ Part of one of the finely carved columns in the great hall at Leptis Magna. Intertwined with the grapevines are scenes from the lives of the god Dionysus and the hero Hercules.

▷ This temple dedicated to "the gods of the city" of Thugga was built by a wealthy local family. The same family also provided the town with a splendid theater.

D   E   F

Leptis Magna – port

Founded possibly as early as the 5th century BC, the town of Leptis Magna was laid out near the harbor, which was well protected from the open sea. The central part of the Roman Empire was far away to the north, but Leptis was connected to it through trade. A lighthouse and a beacon marked the harbor entrance for ships. Produce such as corn and olive-oil was exported from here.

Fine buildings
Wealthy from trade and agriculture, rich citizens of Leptis put up magnificent buildings for the townspeople to use. The Emperor Septimius Severus, who came from Leptis,

△ A carved milestone from Leptis Magna. Its inscription shows that the road goes 44mi inland.

▽ In AD 1 this theater was built in Leptis by a rich nobleman. The columns on the right are part of a temple.

provided the town with a new harbor, a colonnaded forum and an aisled basilica. An imposing street with columns on each side built during the reign of the Emperor Hadrian ran from the harbor to the public baths.

The Emperor Septimius revisited his birthplace in AD 203. To mark the occasion the townspeople erected a great memorial arch at a crossroads which could be seen from all directions.

Today you can stand at the back of the town's theater and look out over the Mediterranean. We can still see a lot of ancient Leptis because its remains were preserved under sand-dunes that gradually engulfed the town.

Timgad – veterans' colony

Unlike Leptis, which was originally founded by the Phoenicians, Timgad was a Roman new town. In AD 100 it was established as a colony for retired soldiers of the Third Legion which was stationed at Lambaesis close by. Like many Roman colonies, it was laid out almost square, like an army fort. Each side was about 385yds long.

Timgad was, in the Roman fashion, divided into regular blocks (called *insulae*). The town had 111 blocks, each of about the same size. This type of town planning helped the early settlers build a well-organized town. It also made it easy for government officials and citizens to find their way through the paved streets. Roman forts were similarly laid out.

Most of the town was taken up with houses for the newly settled army veterans and their families. The original planners did not leave much room for public buildings. You can see the forum and the theater on the aerial photograph. They are built close to the junction of the two main streets, the center of town. There was also a market and a bath building.

Growth and success

To provide all the amenities the citizens wanted, and to house a growing population, Timgad's planners gradually had to build outside the original square site.

These new amenities, which date from the mid-2nd century AD, included another 13 baths, a library, temples, another market just for clothes and a triumphal arch. As the town's population grew, the town council also allowed houses to be built outside the original area. The wall which had at first surrounded the town was taken down, and suburbs grew up to the west and the north. You can see at the top of the photograph the buildings beyond the wall – no longer following the regular, military-style layout.

Timgad's large and thriving population helped to bring peace to this frontier area. The rich farming countryside around Timgad provided the wealth for it to develop.

▷ This photograph of Timgad from the air shows the town's strictly regular plan. The shadows of the rows of columns which lined the two main streets can just be seen.

▽ Timgad's main street. It led to the legionary fort of Lambaesis. A great deal of money went into providing towns with stone-paved roads and colonnaded arcades.

SPAIN – LAND OF GOLD AND SILVER

Early Roman settlements in Spain were in the south and east. When the Emperor Augustus conquered the whole peninsula he divided it into three provinces. Spain quickly became "Romanized", although one army legion remained on duty in the Basque territory in the north in case of rebellion.

Roman Spain's oldest and most famous town was Italica, birthplace of the emperors Trajan and Hadrian. During Hadrian's reign it was redesigned and given colonnaded streets and a large amphitheater.

Mines, wine and fish sauce

"Almost all of Spain has mines producing lead, iron, tin, silver and gold", wrote Pliny in the 1st century AD. There was also copper. The Roman authorities believed that their provinces should produce wealth for the state, and the state owned most of the Spanish mines.

As well as mining, Spain exported huge quantities of olive-oil and wine. It was also famous throughout the Empire for its salted fish sauce, called *garum*, which was exported widely and used in many Roman recipes.

▽ This stone aqueduct brought water to the city of Segovia from Riofrio 10mi away. Its arches stretched nearly a mile to carry the water (at the very top, 100ft above the ground) across the city.

Bay of Biscay

CANTABRIAN MOUNTAINS

Gijón
(Gigia)
(Portus Victoriae)
edo
etum)
León
(Legio)
Retortillo
(Iuliobriga)
Araquil
(Araceli)
PYRENEES
Pamplona
(Pompaelo)
Leiva
(Libia)
SIERRA DE
LA DEMANDA
Calahorra
(Calagurris)
Alfaro
(Graccuris)
Huesca
(Osca)
Vich
(Ausa)
Gerona
(Gerunda)
Sasamon
(Segisamo)
Palencia
(Pallantia)
Tarazona
(Turiasso)
Ebro
Zaragoza
(Caesaraugusta)
Lerida
(Ilerda)
Barcelona
(Barcino)
amora
Ocelum Duri)
Simancas
(Septimanca)
Duero
Osma
(Uxama Argela)
(Bilbilis)
Valderaduey
alamanca
Salmantica)
Arixa
(Arcobriga)
(Segovia)
SERRANIA DE CUENCA
Tortosa
(Dertosa)

△ The highest bridge in
the Roman world was built
at Alcantara over the river
Tagus in AD 106.

SIERRA DE GUADARRAMA
Avila
(Avela)
RA DE GREDOS
Madrid
(Titulcia)
Tagus
Toledo
(Toletum)
Cabeza de Griego
(Segobriga)
(Saguntum)
Talavera la Vieja
(Augustobriga)
Valencia
(Valentia)

Menorca
Pollensa
(Pollentia)
Mahón
(Mago)
Palma
BALEARES
Majorca

Guadiana
(Oretum)
Jucar
Lezuza
(Libisosa)
Denia
(Dianium)
Almaden
(Sisapo)
TARRACONENSIS
(Ad Aras)

■ Province capital
● Other settlement
• Modern town
- - - Province boundary
—— Roman road
Toledo Modern name
(Toletum) Ancient name

Feet
6500
3250
650
0

Alicante
(Lucentum)

Montoro
(Epora)
ETICA
alquivir
Cordoba
(Corduba)
Cartagena
(Carthago Nova)
Ecija
(Astigi)
Martos
(Tucci)
Guadix
(Acci)
Osuna
(Urso)
Genil
Antequera
(Anticaria)
SIERRA NEVADA
Huercal
(Urci)

▷ In the far west of the
Empire, Spain was an
important source of
wealth for the Romans.

Malaga
(Malaca)

Scale 1:3 400 000
0   150 km
0   100 miles

Gibraltar
(Calpe)

57

C   D   E

THE ROMAN TOWN

In AD 331 the people of Orcistus in Galatia asked the Emperor Constantine to grant them the status of a town. The Emperor replied:

"They have declared that in the past their village had all the splendors of a town, appointed officials each year and was filled with people and citizens. Many public roads led to it, there is an adequate supply of water, public and private baths and it is adorned with statues."

Anyone traveling through the Roman Empire would expect to see all towns with much the same facilities for their inhabitants. Early Roman towns developed gradually from earlier foundations, Etruscan or Greek perhaps. In the provinces many completely new towns were established on land not built on before.

The town plan
What made up a Roman town? If it was a new town, or if part of an old one was rebuilt, there would be properly laid-out streets crossing at right angles. These divided the town into regular blocks, *insulae* ("islands").

If the town was rich enough, and was given permission by Rome, it might build a stone wall around as protection. The streets would be paved if possible. Outside the town's limits would be the cemeteries.

Water and sewage
Aqueducts brought fresh water into the town. This was distributed by underground pipes and by fountains. Sewage and waste water (especially from baths) would also be dealt with in the town's plan. Officials were appointed to look after these services.

Public buildings
Most of the town would be taken up with houses, shops and workshops. The most important public area was the forum, the town square. This was where markets were held and business was conducted. Around it there would be law courts, council offices, public halls (basilicas) and temples.

If the town was wealthy there might be a theater and perhaps an amphitheater. There had to be public baths – no town was considered civilized without them.

▽ Herculaneum is close to Pompeii on the Bay of Naples. It was made uninhabitable by the volcanic eruption of Mount Vesuvius in AD 79. Traditionally, the hero-god Hercules founded the town, which dates back to the 6th century BC.

The town was quite small, with a population of around 5,000. It was on the edge of the sea, and archaeologists have found the remains of boats there.

The streets ran back from the sea in blocks.

Herculaneum had some elegant houses of two or three stories with their own gardens and wide views of the bay. Many of the ordinary houses had shops or workshops on the ground floor. Not all the town has been excavated, but the forum, a basilica, a theater, a public bath-house, a gymnasium and a swimming-pool have been found.

▷ Both town and country houses were often finely decorated inside. Walls were painted, and some of the floors were covered with mosaics made from thousands of cubes of colored stone and tile.

In the areas of Gallia and Germania lived a number of Celtic-speaking peoples.

"Nearly all the Gauls are tall, fair-haired and have a ruddy complexion. They are always quarreling and are a proud and insolent people." – Ammianus Marcellinus.

In the far south of Gallia some settlements, such as Massilia, had been established as early as 600 BC by the Greeks. Later Julius Caesar conquered a vast area to the north and created new boundaries for the Roman world in the west, as far as the Atlantic seaboard.

"Long-haired Gaul"

This new area can be divided into three very different parts. In the south the earlier settlements were enlarged and Romanized. Magnificent Roman remains can still be seen in towns such as Nîmes, Arles and Orange. The biggest of the towns in the area was Lyon, and at Narbonne a large port was established.

In the north and west, which the Romans called Gallia Comata ("long-haired Gaul"), the land was open and fertile. Large farming estates filled the well-populated countryside. In Germania, near to the Rhine, new colonies (towns for retired soldiers) were built as well as a line of forts to form a new frontier.

In the late Empire the balance of trading power shifted from the south to the north. This was due to an imperial court at Trier attracting increased financial and material resources.

▷ Many places specialized in particular crafts and exported to the rest of the Empire. This fine-quality glass jug comes from Urdingen.

▽ One of the impressive main gateways in the city walls of Autun. This entrance has two arches for vehicles and two for pedestrians.

◁ Bronze statue of a farm-worker found in Trier. The hooded cloak and woolen leggings provided warmth in the northern winter.

■	Province capital
●	Other settlement
– – –	Province boundary
——	Roman road
Paris	Modern name
(Lutetia)	Ancient name
⨝	Mountain pass

Feet
6500
4900
1300
650
0
Below sea level

▷ The Alps comprise a barrier dividing France from Italy. The Romans would talk about "this side" (their side) or "the other side" of the Alps. In France the earliest Roman towns were in "the Province" – today called Provence.

6

5

4

3

2

1

GERMANIA
INFERIOR

Valkenburg

Nijmegen
(Noviomagus)

Xanten
(Vetera)

Boulogne
(Gesoriacum)

Tournai
(Turnacum)

Tongeren
(Atuatuca)

Neuss
(Novaesium)

Köln
(Colonia Agrippina)

Bonn
(Bonna)

Koblenz
(Confluentes)

English Channel

Cambrai
(Camaracum)

Amiens
(Samarobriva)

Estrées–sur–Noye

Nizy
(Minatiacum)

Meuse

Arlon
(Orolaunum)

BELGICA

Trier
(Augusta Treverorum)

Mosel

Wiesbaden
(Aquae Mattiacae)

*TAURUS
MTS*

Mainz (Moguntiacum)

Worms
(Borbetomagus)

Speyer
(Noviomagus)

Cherbourg
(Coriallum)

Bayeux
(Augustodurum)

Rouen
(Rotomagus)

Lisieux
(Noviomagus)

Beauvais
(Caesaromagus)

Seine

Reims (Durocortorum)

Marne

Metz (Divodurum)

Avranches
(Legedia)

Sées
(Seii)

Paris
(Lutetia)

Chartres
(Autricum)

Troyes
(Augustobona)

Seine

Nijon
(Noviomagus)

Toul
(Tullum)

Strasbourg
(Argentorate)

Baden-Baden
(Aquae)

Neckar

Rhine

Rennes
(Condate)

LUGDUNENSIS

Sens
(Agedincum)

GERMANIA
SUPERIOR

VOSGES MTS

*BLACK
FOREST*

Le Mans
(Suindinum)

Auxerre
(Autessiodurum)

Augst
(Augusta Rauricorum)

Windisch
(Vindonissa)

Angers
(Iuliomagus)

Nantes
(Portus Namnetum)

Tours
(Caesarodunum)

Loire

Avallon
(Aballo)

Dijon
(Dibio)

Besançon (Besontio)

L de Neuchâtel

Bressuire
(Segora)

Bourges
(Avaricum)

Decize
(Decetia)

Autun
(Augustodunum)

Chalon–sur–Saône
(Cavillonum)

*JURA
MTS*

Vevey (Viviscus)

ALPS

Poitiers
(Limonum)

Argenton
(Argentomagus)

Nyons
(Noviodunum)

L Léman

ALPES GRAIAE
ET POENINAE

Rom
(Rauranum)

Néris-les-Bains
(Aquae Neri)

Saône

Geneva

Vienne

Royan
Novioriqum

Limoges
(Augustoritum)

Clermont-Ferrand
(Augustonemetum)

Lyon
(Lugdunum)

Rhône

Aime
(Axima)

Angoulême
(Iculisma)

Feurs
(Forum Segusiavorcum)

Vienne
(Vienna)

Moutiers
(Darantasia)

Isère

Susa
(Segusio)

AQUITANIA

Périgueux
(Vesunna)

*MASSIF
CENTRAL*

Allier

Grenoble
(Culara)

ALPES
COTTIAE

Bordeaux
(Burdigala)

Embrun
(Eburodurum)

Cahors
(Divona)

Lot

Dordogne

Rhône

NARBONENSIS

Digne
(Dinia)

Bazas
(Vasates)

Agen (Aginnum)

Rodez
(Segodunum)

Uzès
(Ucetia)

Orange
(Arausio)

ALPES
MARITIMAE

Garonne

Tarn

Nîmes
(Nemausus)

St Rémy
(Glanum)

Durance

Cimiez
(Cemenelum)

Lectoure
(Lactora)

Adour

Toulouse
(Tolosa)

Lodève
(Luteva)

Arles
(Arelate)

Aix-en-Provence
(Aquae Sextiae)

Antibes
(Antipolis)

Bayonne
(Lapurdum)

Auch
(Elimberris)

Beziers
(Baeterrae)

Marseille
(Massilia)

Fréjus
(Forum Iulii)

Carcassonne
(Carcaso)

Narbonne
(Narbo)

PYRENEES

Castel Roussillon
(Ruscino)

Mediterranean Sea

Scale 1:4 000 000

0 _____ 150 km

0 _____ 100 miles

A   B   C   D

Villa at Estrées-sur-Noye

The aerial photograph and drawing show a villa, or farming estate, at Estrées-sur-Noye in the valley of the river Somme in northern France. It is not far from the town of Amiens, which the Romans called Samarobriva in the province of Gallia. This area has been much surveyed by archaeologists in recent years, mainly from the air, and over a thousand villas have been discovered. The land must have been fertile and well farmed in the Roman period. The villa at Estrées-sur-Noye is like many others found in the same area. Its farm buildings are contained in a walled courtyard 385yds in length. On the photograph a rectangle can be seen near the main gateway. This was probably the site of a small shrine used by the farm workers.

▷ You can see the outline of the buildings clearly because stone and mortar from the walls have been brought to the surface by deep plowing.

▽ A reconstruction of the villa. Notice that the owner's house is set in its own walled garden. The other buildings are for workers and animals, and for storing farm produce and machinery.

Owner's house

Formal gardens

Farm manager's house – also with gardens in front

Cottages or dormitories for farm laborers

Farm entrance – makes the farmyard safe and keeps in the animals

Buildings at Nîmes

The Roman city of Nemausus lies under the modern city of Nîmes in Provence, southern France. It was first a Celtic and then a Greek settlement. The walled Roman city was laid out in 16 BC especially for retired soldiers. In an area which specialized in exporting its quality farm produce it became a very rich city, with a population of about 50,000 in the 2nd century AD. The city is now famous for its Roman remains – the amphitheater below, the aqueduct called Pont du Gard and the temple called Maison Carrée.

▷ This coin celebrates the resettlement of Greeks from Egypt in Nîmes. Nile Crocodiles were "hunted" in amphitheaters.

▽ The amphitheater of Nîmes was built to hold a huge crowd of spectators – as many as 25,000.

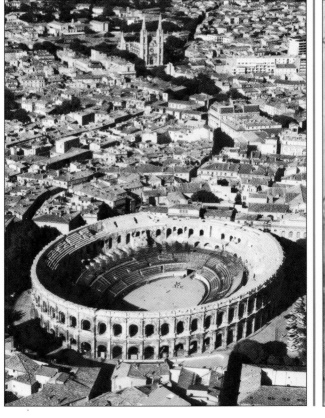

City at Trier

The people who lived in the northeastern part of Gaul were called the Treveri. The Emperor Augustus created a new city at Trier in 15-13 BC and called it Augusta Treverorum ("the city of the Treveri people founded by Augustus"). Much later the Emperor Constantine lived here and built a cathedral, the biggest baths outside Rome itself, a palace and a great basilica. Trier became a major imperial residence. The city declined in the 5th century AD, after repeated attacks by barbarians.

△ This wall painting from Trier may possibly be a portrait of Fausta, wife of Constantine.

◁ The north gate in Trier's city wall, built in the late 2nd century AD, the Porta Nigra or "Black Gate".

▽ Workers outside a country house – a fresco painting from Trier.

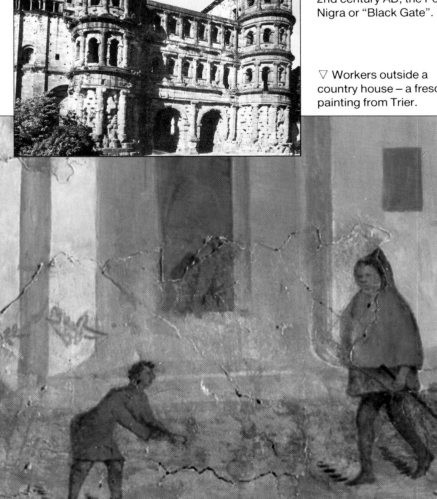

BUILDINGS AND TECHNOLOGY

"City of Rome District III called Isis and Serapis contains... a coin mint; the Colosseum amphitheater which has 45,000 seats; great training school for gladiators; house of Bruttius Prasesens; central theatrical storehouse; Shepherd's Fountain; Baths of Titus and Trajan; Portico of Livia; camp of the sailors of the Misenum fleet; 12 crossroads shrines; 2,757 blocks of apartments; 60 private houses; 18 storehouses; 80 baths; 16 bakeries."

This official catalog of the buildings in one of the 14 districts of Rome was made in the mid-4th century AD. It shows the huge number of buildings, especially blocks of apartments, in just one district of the city. The catalog ends with a summary of the most important buildings and structures in Rome. It includes 28 libraries, 8 bridges, 11 forums, 10 basilicas, 11 public baths, 19 aqueducts and 29 roads.

The Romans could build all this because they were good engineers and architects. They understood how structures stood up and developed the technology to build them. They learned some techniques from other peoples, especially the Etruscans, and they admired the temples and colonnades of the Greeks.

△ This aqueduct, called Pont du Gard, was built in the time of the Emperor Augustus to carry water to the city of Nîmes in Gaul from a source 30mi away.

Section through a road

◁ To build their road network the Romans needed surveyors who understood the landscape and how to measure it. You can see a surveyor here sighting a straight line using an instrument called a *groma*. The Romans tried to make their roads as straight as they could. The road surface was raised above ground level by pounding down layers of stone or gravel or whatever local materials were to hand.

◁ This cross-section through an amphitheater shows how the Romans were able to build tall structures which had to carry enormous weight. The circular series of arches spread out the load – including the weight of 45,000 spectators in the Colosseum.

▽ Just part of the water-powered mills at Barbegal near Arles in Gaul. Eight pairs of large wooden wheels, through a series of gears, drove the millstones. The water came from an aqueduct on top of a hill, and the excess water flowed into a great lake below.

The population of Arles is estimated to have been 80,000 in the early 4th century AD. This great mill must have provided enough flour for all those people. It is still possible to see the remains of the mill building, the water channels and aqueduct.

Roads and communications

The Romans had better routes of communication than any previous people in the Mediterranean. The Empire's road system began at the Great Forum in Rome and was marked by a golden milestone. In the provinces the first roads were built by the army to conquer new lands. A courier on imperial business, traveling by horse, changed horses regularly at official posting-stations and could cover more than 144mi in 24 hours.

Water supply in the towns

The Romans needed a very large supply of water, not just for drinking but for their public baths and lavatories. They brought water to towns in aqueducts (the word means "bringer of water"). In some places these were simple ditches, lined with wood or stone. But many towns had elaborately built stone aqueducts which carried water over long distances.

Inside towns water was collected in basins and tanks and then distributed by underground pipes. A superintendent of the water supply in Rome named Frontinus wrote a manual in about AD 97 describing his work. He estimated that his aqueducts supplied Rome with 260 million gallons every 24 hours.

Mills and other machinery

Although the Romans probably did not use wind power for mills, they did use water power. In many parts of the Empire they built aqueducts to bring the right water pressure to power wheels which drove grindstones to turn corn into flour. Smaller millstones were turned by animals or slaves in the town bakeries.

The Romans invented a number of machines to carry out difficult tasks. The *vallus*, or reaping machine, was pushed by a horse against standing corn. A lifting device with a large wheel was used to take large blocks of stone up to tall structures. Water-clocks were used to time speeches in the law courts. A boat powered by oxen turning paddle-wheels was invented in the 4th century AD but it was never built.

Roman machinery was made of wood and not metal. So it could not withstand constant stress. The gears in the Barbegal water mills (opposite) must have often needed repair.

"The population is very large, and there are very many farmhouses similar to those the Gauls build. There are a large number of cattle. For coins, they use bronze or gold or iron bars. Tin is found inland, and small quantities of iron near the coast. There is also timber of every kind. All the Britons... wear their hair long, and the men have moustaches."

This is part of the description of Britain by Julius Caesar in his book *The War in Gaul*. The Romans were interested in conquering Britain for various reasons. Julius Caesar knew that his newly conquered province of Gaul would not be safe if Celtic trouble-makers could escape to, and plan campaigns from, Britain.

The Romans also wanted to make sure that any new province could not only pay for itself but provide wealth for the central treasury. Caesar wrote about Britain's wealth of metals, and the geographer Strabo saw other possibilities for exports: leather, hunting dogs and a supply of slaves. The province also supplied corn to the Rhine armies.

A series of invasions

Julius Caesar invaded Britain twice, first in 55 and then in 54 BC. He did not leave any troops there. A century later the Emperor Claudius decided to take an interest in what one Roman poet called "far-away Britain". Claudius wanted to win glory for himself by successfully completing a major military campaign.

In AD 43 he came to Britain to join his invasion army of about 40,000 soldiers after they had fought their way to the river Thames. Claudius then led a great procession, with elephants for show, to take possession of the capital Camulodunum (now Colchester).

"Romanization" and prosperity

The Emperor Claudius stayed only 16 days in Britain. The army's commander, Aulus Plautius, stayed on as the province's first governor. His army pushed on, towards the southwest at first, and began to conquer this new territory.

Building roads and forts as they went, the Romans steadily took control of most of England and Wales. But they never managed to conquer the whole island and were forced to build a solid defensive wall in the far north

◁ In times of trouble people buried their wealth. This fine gold belt buckle, made in the late 4th century, was part of the "Thetford hoard" found beside a Roman road in Norfolk.

▽ The Roman army built two permanent northern frontiers. The Emperor Hadrian established the stone wall that bears his name, with its series of forts. Not many years later, the Emperor Antoninus built a turf wall further north.

Fort ◆
Other settlement ●
Roman road —

Netherby (Castra Exploratorum)
Chesters (Cilurnum)
Housesteads (Vercovicium)
Castlesteads
Carvoran (Magnis)
Chesterholm (Vindolanda)
Corbridge (Corstopitum)
Bowness (Maia)
Stanwix
Drumburgh (Congavata)
Carlisle (Luguvalium)

◁ Building inscription from the fort of High Rochester, north of Hadrian's Wall. It records work done by men of the 20th Legion, sent from their base at Chester. The figures represent Mars (god of war) and Hercules with his club.

(Hadrian's Wall). Strong military garrisons were maintained in the north and west.

Apart from parts of mountainous Wales and northern Scotland, the rest of this remote island became "Romanized". The road network grew. Towns developed where Roman army forts had been or on the site of British tribal settlements. Army veterans and their families established colonies. Romans and Britons intermarried. Farmers and villa owners grew rich in the countryside.

GRAMPIAN MOUNTAINS

Tay

Inchtuthil
(Victoria)

ANTONINE WALL

Inveresk
(Coria)

Newstead
(Trimontium)

SOUTHERN UPLANDS

High Rochester
(Aquae Sulis)

Netherby
(Castra Exploratorum)

Corbridge
(Corstopitum)

Wallsend
(Segedunum)

HADRIAN'S WALL

Tyne

CHEVIOT
HILLS

Newcastle
(Pons Aelius)

Bowness
(Maia)

**Carlisle
(Luguvalium)**

Bowes
(Lavatrae)

CUMBRIAN
MTS

Brough
(Verterae)

Tees

Catterick
(Cataractonium)

PENNINES

Ouse

Aldborough
(Isurium)

Irish Sea

Tadcaster
(Calcaria)

■ **York (Eburacum)**

**Brough
(Petuaria)**

Ribchester
(Bremetennacum)

Manchester
(Mamucium)

Buxton
(Aquae Arnemetiae)

Lincoln
(Lindum)

Trent

Chester
(Deva)

Littlechester
(Derventio)

Caernarvon
(Segontium)

Brancaster
(Branodunium)

Willoughby
(Vernemetum)

**Caister
(Venta)**

THE FENS

**Wroxeter
(Viroconium)**

Severn

**Leicester
(Ratae)**

**Water Newton
(Durobrivae)**

Great Ouse

Droitwich
(Salinae)

Godmanchester
(Durovigutum)

Cambridge
(Durolipons)

Avon

Kenchester
(Magnis)

Towcester
(Lactodorum)

CAMBRIAN MTS

Wye

Alcester
(Alauna)

CHILTERN HILLS

Colchester
(Camulodunum)

**Carmarthen
(Moridunum)**

Abergavenny
(Gobarrium)

Gloucester
(Glevum)

St Albans
(Verulamium)

Chelmsford
(Caesaromagus)

**Caerwent
(Venta)**

Thames

**Cirencester
(Corinium)**

**London
(Londinium)** ■

Caeleon
(Isca)

Dorchester
(Durnovaria)

Rochester (Durobrivae)

Bath
(Aquae Sulis)

**Silchester
(Calleva)**

**Canterbury
(Durovernum)**

Richborough
(Rutupiae)

Old Sarum
(Sorviodunum)

**Winchester
(Venta)**

Dover
(Dubris)

**Ilchester
(Lindinis)**

Bitterne
(Clausentum)

**Chichester
(Noviomagus)**

SOUTH DOWNS

Pevensey
(Anderita)

**Dorchester
(Durnovaria)**

Fishbourne

DARTMOOR

**Exeter
(Isca)**

English Channel

North Sea

Province capital ■
Civil capital ▲
Colonia ▼
Other settlement ●
Roman road
Roman road, course uncertain
Roman canal
Roman waterway
Roman wall

Neath — Modern name
(Nidum) — Ancient name
Feet
1625
650
0
Marsh

cale 1:800 000
20 km
15 miles

Wallsend
(Segedunum)

ester
vala)

Newcastle
(Pons Aelius)

South
Shields

ester
omora)

G

Scale 1:2 700 000
0   150 km
0   100 miles

Hadrian's Wall, looking east near the fort at Housesteads.

Street plan at Silchester

Towns in the Roman province of Britain developed in different ways. Some were established where a legion had once been stationed. Others were set up as colonies for retired soldiers. The Romans also encouraged settlements of the native tribes to develop into Romanized towns.

In Hampshire the settlement of the Atrebates tribe was at a place known to the Romans as Calleva Atrebatum ("the town in the woods of the Atrebates"). Calleva, modern Silchester, became the capital of the region under Roman rule.

Calleva was laid out in the usual Roman way, with straight streets crossing at right angles. Around AD 200 a new town wall was built of stone.

The town had the usual public buildings needed to establish a Roman way of life among people who had not experienced it before. The forum was right at the center where the main streets crossed. On one side of it was the basilica for the law courts, meetings and ceremonies. Calleva had no theater, but there was an amphitheater outside the walls, as well as public baths and several temples. About 3,000 people probably lived in the town.

△ Calleva stood at a major crossroads in southern Britain. Near the road to Venta (Winchester) was a lodging-house. Such buildings were situated on main roads throughout the province. The town had fewer buildings near the walls than at the center, so it was probably not heavily populated.

◁ This aerial view of Silchester shows how archaeologists have been able to locate the streets of the town. Their hard stony surfaces have turned the crops in the fields a different color.

Palace at Fishbourne

The magnificent Roman palace at Fishbourne in Sussex must have been very costly to build. Who could have afforded to build it?

The king of the pre-Roman tribe called the Regni had been friendly towards Rome and helped the Emperor Claudius in his invasion of Britain. This king, named Cogidubnus, was rewarded by the Romans for his support. He was allowed to remain king of the area and became a Roman citizen, probably ruling from the town of Noviomagus (Chichester).

Archaeologists think that a large villa-style building was put up at Fishbourne a few years after Claudius' invasion of AD 43. In about AD 75 it was most likely Cogidubnus who had the site landscaped and a huge palace and gardens built. People coming to the palace by road from Chichester, or by boat, would have entered an enclosed,

◁ This 2nd-century AD mosaic floor was probably laid by several mosaic craftsmen in charge of a number of workers. The center picture shows Cupid (with wings and a three-pronged spear) riding a dolphin. Sea-horses, great jars and scallop shells fill the other panels.

△ Archaeologists have excavated nearly all the palace at Fishbourne. This model shows how impressive the building and garden were. The owner – thought to be Cogidubnus (who had Romanized his name) – wanted to show that he really could live like a Roman.

formally laid-out garden, through a grand hallway. The palace was built around the garden, with private wings and a bath block.

Many of the rooms were heated with underfloor heating (the "hypocaust") and were finely decorated with wall paintings and mosaics. Craftsmen such as masons and carpenters probably came from Rome to work on the palace, but we also know from an inscription that there was a craft association in Chichester. There must have been plenty of work on the new Roman-style buildings. A new hypocaust was built only a few years before the palace burned to the ground in the late 3rd century AD.

THE ROMAN VILLA

"Whenever I'm worn out with worry and want to get some rest, I go to my villa," wrote the poet Martial.

The Romans used the word *villa* to mean either a simple farm, a large country estate employing hundreds of workers, a house in the country or a seaside holiday home. Many rich Romans had farming estates scattered through the Empire which brought them wealth from corn, vines or olives. They might also have houses in the mountains or by the seaside.

Working farms

We know about Roman farms from those which have been excavated by archaeologists. The villa at Settefinestre (opposite) is one which has been carefully examined. We also know about farms from Roman writers such as Columella. In his book *About Farming* he wrote:

"A farm should be in a place with a healthy climate, with fertile soil, with some flat ground and some hilly, on an eastern or southern slope – but not too steep. The villa should have three sections: the 'villa urbana', the house of the owner; the 'villa rustica', the house of the farm manager and labourers; and the 'villa fructuaria', the storehouses."

Country houses

Whether the owner's house was part of a large farm building as at Settefinestre or a country or seaside home, a Roman expected all the amenities of a town house. The *atrium*, or enclosed courtyard, had various rooms around it – some were bedrooms, and one would be the *tablinum* or main living-room. There might be several *triclinia*, or dining-rooms, around the house to catch the afternoon sun throughout the year.

In town a family would visit the public baths. In their house in the country they would have their own set of bathrooms inside the house or in a separate block outside.

Villas of the north

The Roman villa was more important to the economy in the northern Empire – Britain and Gaul – than in the Mediterranean region. The heavy soil of the north was suitable for the large-scale agriculture that could make villa farmers rich.

△ We could easily use the modern word "villa" for this luxury seaside home from a wall painting found at Pompeii. A number of these looked out over the Bay of Naples.

▷ The main building of this estate is on a slope, with formal gardens laid out in front. The living areas are built on top of the hill and the cellars (through the arches).

Behind the colonnades on the front of the first floor were the family rooms, baths and wine and oil presses. The manager and slaves lived at the back of the house.

Villa rustica

Courtyard

Farmyard

Domus
(home)

Garden

Garden

Turreted garden

Garden

◁ Not everyone lived in grand villas. This mosaic shows a North African country worker pouring wine from a goatskin outside his traditional thatched hut.

▷ Groundplan of the great villa at Settefinestre. The villa was the center of a large estate built in the 1st Century B.C. near the colony of Cosa in Etruna (central Italy).

The site, which has been extensively excavated since 1974, shows that the main crop of the large farm was wine produced using slaves who worked under a farm manager.

THE DANUBE – BARBARIAN FRONTIERS

The provinces of Germany and those just south of the Danube were the "front-line states" of the Roman Empire. To the north were the peoples the Romans called *barbari*, mimicking the sound of their speech. These barbarians neither spoke Latin nor lived like the Romans.

Natural frontier

The river Danube provided a good natural frontier, but many legionary forts were built on its southern banks. Soldiers were recruited in these northern provinces to fight in other parts of the Empire.

At the weak point in the northern defense, between the rivers Rhine and Danube, a permanent barrier with a patrol road was built – it was called the *limes*. The Black Sea provided the Empire's northeastern boundary.

By AD 106 the Roman army had pushed north and conquered the new province of Dacia (now part of Romania). Towns and colonies for army veterans and their families were built there.

Growth of towns

The legionary forts of the Danube region were places where traders, as well as soldiers' families, came to live. Small villages, known as *canabae*, developed and eventually became proper Roman towns. At Split on the Adriatic Sea the Emperor Diocletian built a seaside palace for his retirement.

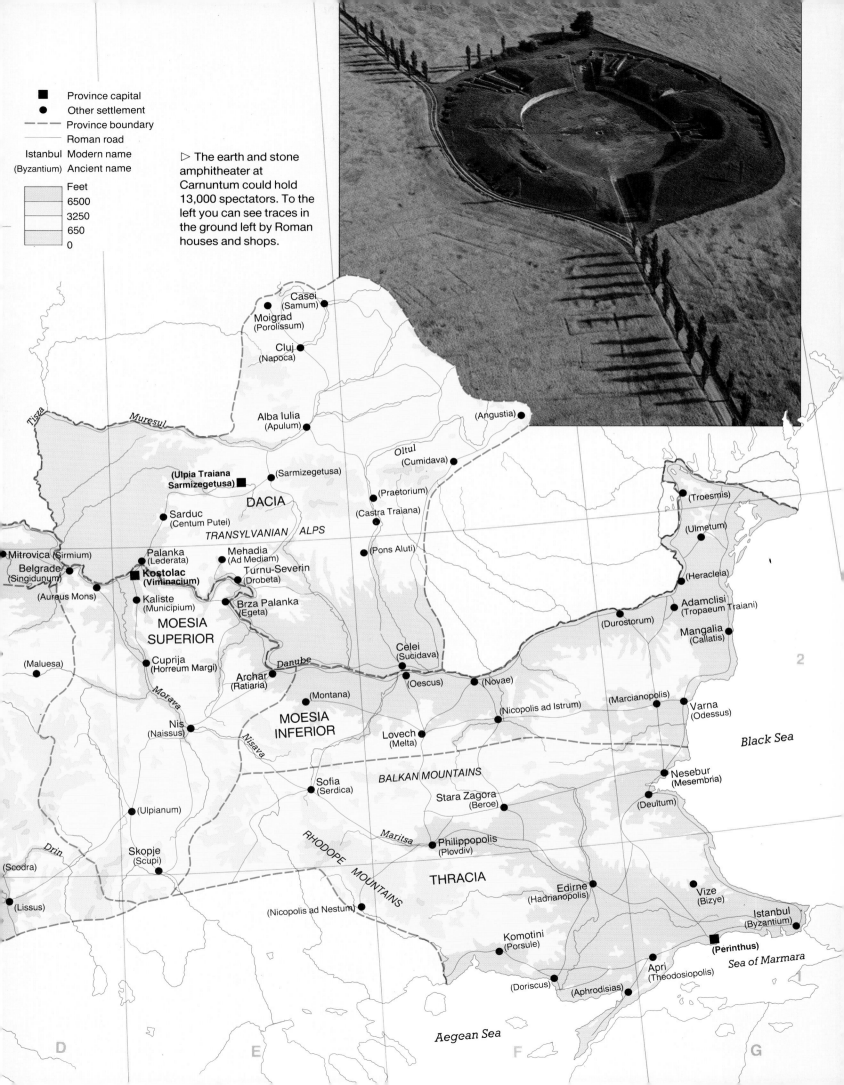

Legend

■ Province capital
● Other settlement
- - - Province boundary
—— Roman road
Istanbul Modern name
(Byzantium) Ancient name

Feet
6500
3250
650
0

▷ The earth and stone amphitheater at Carnuntum could hold 13,000 spectators. To the left you can see traces in the ground left by Roman houses and shops.

Tisza

Muresul

Casei
(Samum)
Moigrad
(Porolissum)

Cluj
(Napoca)

Alba Iulia
(Apulum)

(Angustia)

Oltul

(Cumidava)

(Ulpia Traiana
Sarmizegetusa) ■
(Sarmizegetusa)

DACIA

(Praetorium)

(Troesmis)

Sarduc
(Centum Putei)

(Castra Traiana)

(Ulmetum)

TRANSYLVANIAN ALPS

Mitrovica (Sirmium)

Palanka
(Lederata)
Mehadia
(Ad Mediam)

(Pons Aluti)

Belgrade
(Singidunum)

Kostolac
(Viminacium)

Turnu-Severin
(Drobeta)

(Heracleia)

(Aureus Mons)

Kaliste
(Municipium)

Brza Palanka
(Egeta)

(Durostorum)

Adamclisi
(Tropaeum Traiani)

MOESIA
SUPERIOR

Mangalia
(Callatis)

Celei
(Sucidava)

(Maluesa)

Cuprija
(Horreum Margi)

Danube

Archar
(Ratiaria)

(Oescus)

(Novae)

Morava

(Montana)

(Marcianopolis)

Varna
(Odessus)

MOESIA
INFERIOR

Nis
(Naissus)

Nisava

Nicopolis ad Istrum)

Lovech
(Melta)

Black Sea

BALKAN MOUNTAINS

Nesebur
(Mesembria)

Sofia
(Serdica)

Stara Zagora
(Beroe)

Deultum)

(Ulpianum)

RHODOPE

Maritsa

Philippopolis
(Plovdiv)

Drin

Skopje
(Scupi)

MOUNTAINS

THRACIA

Edirne
(Hadrianopolis)

Vize
(Bizye)

(Scodra)

Nicopolis ad Nestum)

Istanbul
(Byzantium)

(Lissus)

Komotini
(Porsule)

(Perinthus) ■

Sea of Marmara

Apri
(Theodosiopolis)

(Doriscus)

(Aphrodisias)

Aegean Sea

2

D   E   F   G

GREECE – AN ANCIENT CIVILIZATION

Greek language and culture
The Romans admired Greek civilization.

"I prefer that a boy should learn Greek as his first language. He will soon pick up Latin, whether he likes it or not, as it is in general use" – Quintilian.

The author of the above quotation, Quintilian, became the first Roman "university professor" in Athens. He was also tutor to the Emperor Vespasian's children. Rich Romans sent their sons (but not their daughters) to Athens to complete their education.

Three provinces of Greece
The Romans divided Greece into three provinces, with a governor in charge of each. Achaea in the south was still the centre of the old Greek civilization. Under the Romans several of its cities and sacred places such as Delphi were restored and rebuilt.

Much of this restoration and building went on in the 2nd century AD. A wealthy Athenian named Herodes Atticus was responsible for a

△ This delicate carving in marble shows Christ as the Greek god Apollo playing the lyre.

▽ Part of the Roman road called Via Egnatia between Philippi and Neapolis in Macedonia. The edging stones can be seen clearly.

variety of public buildings – a theater in Athens, an aqueduct at Olympia, a stadium at Delphi and healing pools for the sick at Thermopylae.

In the north, Thessalonica became the provincial capital of Macedonia. It was an important port on the route to the eastern Empire. It became a Roman colony in the middle of the 3rd century and was enlarged in the 5th century, when its town walls and a new palace were built.

Early Christianity
Greece under the Romans is also associated with Christianity. It was to Greece that St Paul came on his second journey. He was arrested at the Roman colony of Philippi after a riot and was only released when he was discovered to be a Roman citizen. Paul later preached in Athens and Corinth.

▽ About half of the 5mi length of the 5th-century walls of Thessalonica still survives.

Durrës
(Epidamnus)

Ohrid
(Lychnidus)

Bitola
(Heraclea Lyncestis)

L Ohridsko

L Prespansko

(Apollonia)

Vijose

MACEDONIA

(Stobi)

Crna

Axios

(Aegae)
(Pella)

Strimon

Kavalla
(Neapolis)

(Amphipolis)
(Philippi)

(Thasos)

Thasos

(Samothracia)

Samothraki

Saloniki
(Thessalonica)

KHALKIDHIKI

(Beroea)

(Oricum)

Sarande
(Onchesmus)

Aliakmon

(Dium)

Mt Olympus

(Potidaea)

(Hephaestia)

Lemnos

Corfu
(Corcyra)

Corfu

(Dodona)

EPIRUS

Trikkala
(Tricca)

Pinios

(Larisa)

(Metropolis)

(Demetrias)

Northern
Sporades

Aegean
Sea

Ionian
Islands

(Nicopolis)

(Ambracia)

PINDUS
MTS

Skiros

Levkas

(Stratus)

Thermopylae

(Aedepsus)

Ionian
Sea

(Naupactus)

(Naryca)

Halae

Euboea

(Anthedon)

Sami
(Same)

Kefallinia

Patras
(Patrae)

ACHAEA

(Delphi)

Levadhia
(Lebadea)

Thisvi
(Thisbe)

Thebes
(Thebae)

(Marathon)

(Eleusis)

PELOPONNESE

(Sicyon)

Corinth
(Corinthus)

(Isthmia)

Athens
(Athenae)

(Piraeus)

(Geraestus)

Andros

■ Province capital
● Other settlement
○ Important ruin
△ Mountain
≍ Mountain pass
– – – Province boundary
—— Roman road
Athens Modern name
(Athenae) Ancient name

(Olympia)

Zakinthos

Alfios

(Argos)

(Mantinea)

(Mycenae)

Aiyina

△Mt Laurium

Tinos

(Tinos)

(Asine)

(Troezen)

Cyclades

(Megalopolis)

△Mt Ithomi

Paros

Sifnos

(Naxos)

Messini
(Messene)

Sparti
(Sparta)

Naxos

Feet

6500
3250
650
0

Milos

(Teuthrone)

(Asopus)

Scale 1:2 500 000

0   120 km
0   80 miles

Kithira

Thera

(Thera)

A   B   C   D

3

2

1

Athens – city of splendor

Much of ancient Athens was destroyed by the armies of the consul Sulla in the 1st century BC. Several Roman emperors later rebuilt and added to the city, recreating the glory of this center of classical Greek civilization. Both Julius Caesar and the Emperor Augustus put up public buildings. The Emperor Hadrian carried out many public works. The millionaire Herodes Atticus built an odeum, or concert theater, that held more than 5,000 people.

The Emperor Hadrian in Athens
Hadrian first visited Athens in AD 124-5 and by the end of his reign in AD 138 he had almost transformed the city. He completed a huge temple to the Greek god Zeus (called Jupiter by the Romans) which had been started long before in the 6th century BC. He built a temple dedicated to all the Greeks. During his three winters in Athens, Hadrian also saw work finished on an aqueduct, a gymnasium, a huge library and a bridge.

On a triumphal arch the Emperor built there are two inscriptions. On one side it reads, "This is Athens, the ancient city of Theseus", but on the other, "This is the city of Hadrian and not of Theseus."

▷ Inside this 1st-century BC "Tower of the Winds" was a 24-hour clock driven by water power. It is decorated with wall sculptures showing the "eight winds".

▽ Part of a statue of the Emperor Hadrian, with the Acropolis in the background. His breast-plate shows the she-wolf with Romulus and Remus, and figures representing Victory.

△ The Acropolis of Athens, with the Parthenon, the Greek temple of the city's goddess. On the slope below is the odeum of Herodes Atticus.

Corinth – destroyed and then rebuilt

Corinth was a wealthy and important city in the Greek world. One Roman writer described it as "that beautiful city full of treasures of every kind".

In the middle of the 2nd century BC Corinth tried to fight against the Romans along with other cities in Achaea. The result was terrible for Corinth. The Roman consul Lucius Mummius was sent to Greece with a large fleet and an army. He completely destroyed Corinth (setting it on fire), made all of its people slaves and carried off all its art treasures.

More than 100 years later Julius Caesar chose the site of Corinth to establish a colony for retired soldiers from Italy. He set about reconstructing some of the ruined buildings and planning a new city, complete with an impressive city center. Roman Corinth became a major trading and business center.

Restoring the Greek city
Standing above every other building in Corinth was the temple to the Greek god Apollo. Built in the 6th century BC, it was restored by the Romans. The approach to the city center was along a wide road (later called the Lechaeum Road) that ran more than a third of a mile from the harbor. Entry from that road into the forum or *agora* (as the Greeks called it) was by way of a grand triumphal arch. The forum was the town's main business area and was surrounded by a number of colonnaded buildings.

Some of the most important buildings here were the basilicas. These large halls were used for meetings and law courts. Corinth was the capital city of Greece in Roman times, so there was a lot of business and administration for the governor and officials to carry out.

The 2nd-century AD millionaire Herodes Atticus paid for an odeum to be built at Corinth, as well as one in Athens. Cut into the rock, this small theater could seat an audience of 3,000.

Corinth was destroyed a second time by an earthquake in AD 521.

△ Stone seats at the theater at Corinth. Built originally by the Greeks, it was remodeled by the Romans.

▽ Plan of Roman Corinth. The Romans added a number of temples to the city center.

The Corinth canal
One of the sights of modern Greece is the canal which joins the Gulf of Corinth to the Aegean Sea. Julius Caesar wanted to build a canal. The Emperor Caligula surveyed the ground, and the Emperor Nero actually started digging in AD 67 – or rather his 6,000 Jewish war-slaves did. The modern canal was completed in 1893.

Map labels: theater, to amphitheater, Lechaeum road, north market, baths of Eurycles, odeum, temple of Apollo, basilica, peribolos of Apollo, Julian basilica, northwest stoa, temple, Glauce fountain, shops, sacred fountain, monumental arch, fountain of Peirene, agora, speakers' platform, temples, temple, shops, south stoa, council house, south basilica

0   100 m
0   300 ft

ASIA MINOR – WHERE EAST MET WEST

The Romans first became interested in Asia Minor during the reign of the Seleucid King Antiochus III. He was defeated by the Romans in two land battles and one at sea in 190 BC. Three other kings gave their territories to the Romans. This left only Lycia and Cilicia for the Romans to conquer.

Pirates

These areas were well known for being the haunt of pirates who lived on land but hunted down ships traveling in this part of the Mediterranean. After many campaigns against them they were crushed by Pompey the Great in 67 BC.

There were a number of important Greek cities already established before the Roman occupation, especially along the coast. The Emperor Augustus set up most of the Roman colonies in Asia Minor – for example, at Antiochia, Olbasa and Iconium. Augustus built a special road to link these new colonies. Elsewhere the Romans used and improved on the road system which already existed.

Roman Cyprus

Until Cyprus was made Roman in 58 BC it had been part of Egyptian territory for nearly 250 years. The capital of the island was Paphus, but the port of Salamis became the biggest city and main center of trade. The Romans exported much of the island's raw materials – timber and copper (from the state mines) – and corn. Those who exploited Cyprus became rich, but the island gradually suffered as a result.

◁ This colorful mosaic was made in the 4th century for a house in the town of Curium on the south coast of Cyprus. There is also a well-preserved theater near by.

Scale 1:3 800 000

0   200 km

0   150 miles

■ Province capital
● Other settlement
--- Province boundary
— Roman road
Samsun Modern name
(Amisus) Ancient name

Feet
6500
3250
650
0

Sinop
(Sinope)

Inebolu
(Abonuteichus)

(Amastris) ■

PONTINE   MOUNTAINS

Black Sea

Samsun
(Amisus)

(Side)

Trapezus)

Eregli
(Heraclea Pontica)

(Eupatoria)

(Claudiopolis)

(Gangra)

(Amasea)

Kelkit

(Comana Pontica)

Satala)

Nicopolis)

Ankara
(Ancyra) ■

(Tavium)

Sivas
(Megalopolis)

Euphrates

(Pessinus)

CAPPADOCIA

Kizil Irmak

*Tuz
Gölü*

**Kayseri
(Mazaca)** ■

GALATIA

Malatya
(Melitene)

(Garsaura)

(Cucusus)

*Beyşehir
Gölü*

(Tyana)

Konya
(Iconium)

(Podandus)

(Anazarbus)

(Isaura)

Karaman
(Laranda)

Ataniya
(Adana)

(Issus)

CILICIA

(Tarsus) ■

(Soli)

TAURUS   MOUNTAINS

Selimiye
(Side)

(Claudiopolis)

Silifke
(Seleucia)

(Elaeusa)

Gazipasa
(Selinus)

(Carpasia)

Lapithos
(Lapethus)

Cyprus

(Limenia)

(Tamassus)

(Salamis)

Paphus ■

Larnaca
(Citium)

(Curium)

(Amathus)

Ephesus – Asian capital

When King Attalus III gave his kingdom to the Romans in his will in 133 BC, the city of Ephesus became the capital of the new province of Asia and the governor lived here. It had already been a wealthy city under the Greeks and was famous for its temple to the goddess Artemis, one of the Seven Wonders of the World in ancient times. Originally on the sea (the coastline has now moved), Ephesus was an important port.

During the Greek period a wall enclosed the city and connected it with the harbor and the coast. An impressive road lined with

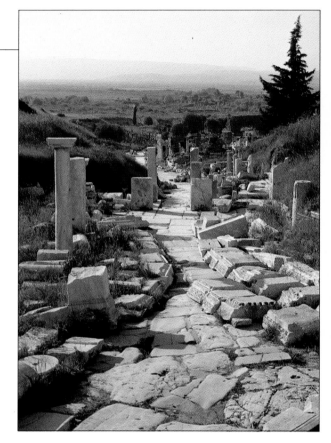

▷ It was along this paved road that the procession for the festival of Artemis (called Diana by the Romans) led from her temple to the theater.

◁ Impressive entrance to the temple of the Emperor Hadrian, built in the early 2nd century AD. Emperors were often worshiped as gods, especially away from Rome.

▽ If you were rich enough you could afford a grand town house like this in the city center. The walls of this room are painted to make it look as if they are covered with marble.

columns (rather like the Lechaeum Road in Corinth) ran from the harbor to the theater. This theater was first built in the 3rd century BC. Roman rebuilding, begun in AD 41, took 80 years to complete. Afterwards the theater held about 25,000 spectators. The city was also famous for its library, which was built during the 2nd century AD in honor of Celsus, one of the governors.

St Paul in Ephesus
St Paul, on his third journey, visited Ephesus and caused a riot there. His Christian teachings particularly upset the silversmiths who made offerings for those who worshiped the goddess Artemis.

A silversmith called Demetrius addressed a huge crowd in the city's theater, complaining about the disrespect to their goddess and lack of trade. The crowd shouted: "Great is Artemis, goddess of the people of Ephesus!" The town clerk had to calm the crowds and tell them that they could make official complaints to the governor.

Aphrodisias – theater, temple and baths

The name of this city comes from its patron goddess Aphrodite. She was the Greek goddess of love and beauty, called Venus by the Romans. Aphrodisias was a popular visiting place both with 1st-century BC generals such as Sulla and Julius Caesar and with the emperors Augustus and Hadrian.

Aphrodite's temple here was built in the 1st century BC. In the 2nd century AD the Emperor Hadrian had a special courtyard put up around it. In the 6th century, like many Greek and Roman temples, it became a Christian church.

This was an important area for the supply of fine-quality marble. Marble from Aphrodisias was exported to many parts of the Roman world. It was also a city noted for its arts, especially stone carving. The influence of artists working at Aphrodisias spread as far as North Africa.

City entertainments

In the 2nd century AD the great theater was converted so that it could be used as an amphitheater – for gladiator shows and wild-beast fights. There were also other buildings for public entertainment.

Just in front of the temple of Aphrodite is the site of the odeum, where concerts and recitals took place. The city also had a stadium for athletics and chariot racing. (Now under grass, the site is at the very top of the aerial photograph.) In about AD 265 a defensive wall was built around the stadium, but excluding the rest of the city.

Another favorite Roman pastime was going to the public baths. Hadrian built a very large bath block for the people of Aphrodisias. (Its remains are on the far left of the photograph.)

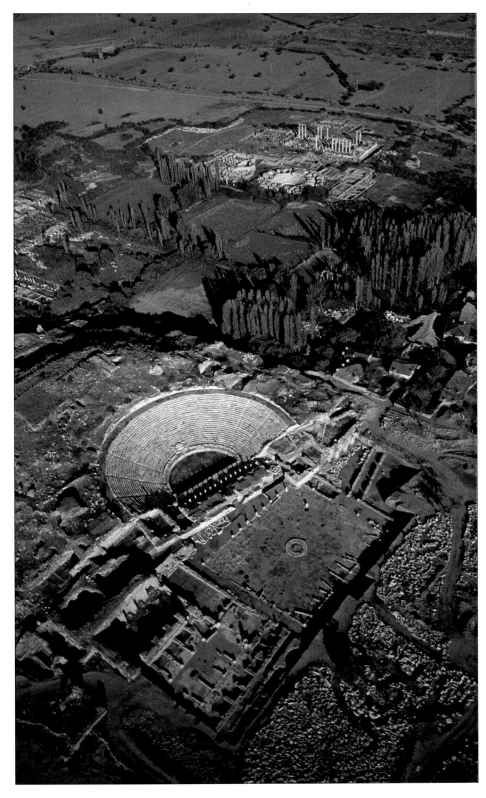

▷ This aerial view of Aphrodisias shows the theater built into the slope of the natural high point of the Greek town – the acropolis. At the top of the picture you can see the tall columns of Aphrodite's temple. At the bottom right are piles of stones from the excavations. There is still much to be discovered here by archaeologists.

TOWN AND CITY LIFE

"There's no peace or quiet in the city for the poor. Early in the morning schoolmasters stop us from having any normal life. Before it gets light we have the bakers. Then it's the hammering of the coppersmiths all day."

This is how the poet Martial described living in Rome. Another writer, Juvenal, mentioned narrow streets "jammed with carts and their swearing drivers, crowded with people pushing and shoving, pavements and roads filthy underfoot".

Roman towns and cities were certainly crowded. Shops, craftspeople and shouting traders filled the streets.

How people shopped

Shops advertised their goods with painted signs (such as a leg of pork for a butcher) or a written notice. All towns had *thermopolia* – hot food for a quick snack on the premises or to take away. Many businesses were family-run, often with slave assistants and young apprentices.

Goods and food were not pre-packaged. You bought your bread at the place where it was first ground into flour, then made into dough and finally baked. If you wanted a pair of sandals, the cobbler would make them for you on the spot. Knives and other tools were made and sold by the ironmonger at his shop.

Housing conditions

Martial and Juvenal complained about the living conditions of the poor in towns. They lived mostly in run-down blocks of apartments, often above shops. In Rome these might be six stories high – although this was less common in other towns. Mostly built of wood, these apartments often burnt to the ground.

People who were rich were able to get some quiet in town. In Rome they built their homes away from the bustling streets, up on the hillsides. Houses of the well-to-do were enclosed, with tucked-away private courtyards. They were cool in the summer and had their own kitchen, dining-room, bedrooms, slave quarters and back garden.

Streets

Under the streets went the sewage and water pipes. Water usually poured into stone basins or troughs at the edge of the road. Most people, who did not have a private water supply, collected their water from these troughs.

In many towns the roads, and sometimes the pavements, were paved with stone.

◁ A shopkeeper reaches up to a shelf behind her. We have evidence of Roman daily life from sculpture such as these memorials on the tombs of shopkeepers and craftspeople from various parts of the Empire.

△ A lady sits with her shopping list written on a wax tablet waiting for the butcher to prepare her order. Notice the weighing scales on the right, the three-legged chopping-block and the hanging joints of meat.

▷ Street life in a Roman town. *"We live in a city shored up with slender props – for that's how the landlords stop the houses from falling down. The place to live is where there are no fires"* – Juvenal.

THE EXOTIC EAST

The area which became the eastern provinces of the Roman Empire was originally ruled by a number of kings. The Romans often made treaties with them and then took over the government of the area.

This happened first of all in Judaea in AD 6, although the Romans did not take full control of this area until AD 44. Even then the Jews of Judaea often rebelled against Roman rule. Syria became Roman in AD 64, Arabia in 106 and Mesopotamia in 114.

Keeping the Roman peace

The Emperor Trajan established a frontier to the Empire on the eastern edge of Arabia and Syria. A network of stone-paved roads was laid across the desert, and soldiers occupied strongly built forts. These forts were often square, with large round towers at each corner. Trajan sent six legions to occupy this area and pacify the peoples. The presence of so many soldiers, their forts and their roads helped establish trade between this area and Rome.

Trade with the east

Many goods were exported from the east to other parts of the Roman Empire: timber, cloth, glass and leather goods, for example. The port of Tyrus was well known for its purple dye which the Romans used for their clothes. The Romans also used a lot of sweet-smelling substances such as frankincense and myrrh for incense, perfume and medicine.

Much of this trade was through Arabia, with the goods carried by camel. A camel train could cover about 20mi in a day, according to Roman writers. There was even trade across the desert with India (for spices) and beyond that with China (for silk). Along with this trade, many easterners came west to Rome.

Wild animals

Many provinces provided exotic animals for "sport" and slaughter in amphitheaters all over the Empire, but especially for Rome itself. The town of Hierapolis in northern Syria became the depot where animals were collected and shipped south – beasts such as tigers, lions, leopards and wild asses. They probably traveled to the Egyptian port of Alexandria for shipment to Rome.

▷ The remains of the massive 1st-century AD temple to the chief god Jupiter at Heliopolis (now Baalbek) in the province of Syria.

▷ View from the citadel or hilltop fortress at Edessa in Mesopotamia.

▽ This mosaic from a tomb in Edessa shows a rich family. Although it is a Roman province, they wear their traditional clothes, and their names are written in the regional language, Syriac.

Samsat
(Samosata)

(Antinonopolis)

TUR ABDIN

Urfa
(Edessa)

■ **Nusaybin**
(Nisibis)

(Zeugma)

Harran
(Carrhae)

Euphrates

(Alexandria ad Issum)

(Cyrrhus)

MESOPOTAMIA

(Singara)

Membij
(Hierapolis)

Aleppo
(Beroea)

■ **Antakya**
(Antiochia)

Raqqa (Nic Horium)

Euphrates

Orontes

SYRIA

Risafe
(Resapha)

Khabir

(Laodicea)

(Apamea)

(Seriane)

Buseire
(Circesium)

Mediterranean Sea

Hama
(Epiphania)

(Raphanaea)

(Dura-Europus)

Tripoli
(Tripolis)

Homs
(Emesa)

(Palmyra)

(Danaba)

SYRIAN DESERT

Beirut
(Berytus)

Baalbek
(Heliopolis)

■ Province capital

● Other settlement

- - - Province boundary

Roman road

Saida
(Sidon)

Damascus

Homs   Modern name

(Emesa) Ancient name

Tyre
(Tyrus)

Feet

(Caesarea Paneas)

6500

3250

*Sea of
Galilee*

650

0

(Tiberias)

El Qanawat
(Canatha)

Below sea level

Nazareth

- - - Seasonal river

(Lejjun)

Um Qeis
(Gadara)

(Caesarea Maritima) ■

(Scythopolis)

■ **Busra**
(Bostra)

(Neapolis)

Jarash
(Gerasa)

Tel Aviv-Yafo
(Joppa)

JUDAEA

(Diospolis)

Jericho

Amman
(Philadelphia)

(Ascalon)

Bethlehem

Jerusalem
(Aelia Capitolina)

Gaza

(Herodion)

(Madaba)

Hebron

*Dead
Sea*

(Masada)

Beersheba
(Berosaba)

Karnak
(Characmoba)

ARABIA

▷ A mosaic from a villa
near Antiochia. It could be
called "Still Life with Boiled
Eggs". Mosaics can tell
us about everyday life
long ago.

(Nessana)

(Oboda)

NEGEV DESERT

(Petra)

Scale 1:3 500 000

0   120 km

0   100 miles

Elat
(Aila)

87

Oasis city at Palmyra

"The tax collector shall exact... for a camel-load of dried foodstuffs...for purple wool by the fleece...for myrrh imported in goat-skins...for each donkey-load of olive-oil" – customs regulations, Palmyra, AD 137.

Palmyra was an oasis (a fertile spot) in the Syrian desert. It was a caravan city. Camel and donkey trains bringing luxury goods from India, China and Arabia passed through Palmyra on their way to coastal ports such as Tyrus and Sidon.

▽ The ruins of the oasis of Palmyra. Beyond the trees of the fertile area lies the desert. Caravans passed this way to and from the river Euphrates and the Persian Gulf.

Magnificent buildings
In the middle of the 2nd century AD a whole series of public buildings was started. Most impressive was the wide street lined with columns which ran nearly half a mile across the city.

The buildings on the edge of the city include an enormous temple to the god Bel. There were other temples dedicated to the locally worshiped gods. The forum of the city must have served as a place for the caravans to load and unload.

Masada

The Jewish people were involved in several rebellions against rule by foreigners. In AD 66 they rose up in arms against the Roman troops stationed in Jerusalem. Rome then sent an army of around 50,000 men to crush the rebellion. Jerusalem was recaptured in AD 70. Large numbers of people died.

The Romans may have thought the rebellion was over. But one Jewish group, called the Zealots, continued the fight. In AD 66 they had taken over the mountain fortress of Masada. We have a vivid account of the siege seven years later from the Jewish historian who called himself Josephus.

Mountain siege

Josephus describes how the Roman army commander, Flavius Silva, built a great ramp against the mountain so his army could break in: "On top of this ramp they constructed a pier of stones and on that built a tower 90 feet high protected all over with plates of iron."

Despite their fortified position, the Jews knew they could not hold out against the Roman army: 960 of them chose suicide rather than surrender. A woman and her five children who hid in a water cistern gave the account of Masada's last days to Josephus.

▽ Herodion, King Herod's fortified mountain-top palace, from the air. Notice the four round towers in the perimeter walls.

▷ View of Masada with (on the left) the ramp built by the Romans. Traces of the square Roman army camps are visible.

EGYPT – ROME'S GRANARY

Egypt was conquered by King Alexander the Great of Macedonia (now part of Greece) in 330 BC. Alexander founded the city of Alexandria, which grew into a great center of Greek culture and influence. After his death a Macedonian general called Ptolemy established himself as king. After him all Egyptian kings were called Ptolemy.

Last of the Ptolemies

The Romans became interested in Egypt in the 2nd century BC, and gradually began to assert their authority there. By the 1st century BC a Ptolemy was only on the throne of Egypt because the Romans wanted him there.

When the Ptolemy who was nicknamed Auletes ("Flute-player") died, his will named his daughter, Cleopatra, and his son, Ptolemy, to succeed him jointly. But he appointed Rome as their guardians. In 30 BC the Emperor Augustus "added Egypt to the Empire of the Roman people".

Corn for Rome

The capital and main port of Egypt, Alexandria, was the second largest city in the Roman Empire. From here the province exported huge quantities of corn. Rome needed these supplies – more than 200,000 Romans registered for free corn in 2 BC. With the annual flooding of the river Nile, Egypt was fertile enough to provide this and all it needed for its own population of about 7 million. Exports from Egypt also included papyrus (for writing on: the Romans did not have paper), flax for making cloth, perfumes, medicines, olives and dates.

Cyrenaica and Crete

Cyrenaica, 500mi to the west of Egypt along the North African coast, became a Roman province in 74 BC. It had originally been an area of Greek colonies and was now governed together with Crete. The most important city was Cyrene. The city was badly damaged in AD 115 during the Jewish Revolt but was restored with the help of the Emperor Hadrian.

Crete, home of the ancient Minoan civilization, was conquered by the Romans in 69-67 BC. It was prosperous during the Roman period, and there were many country villas on the island.

Marsa Susah
(Apollonia)

Tulmaythah
(Ptolemais)

Tukrah
(Tauchira)

Shahhat
(Cyrene)

Derna
(Darnis)

(Barca)

Benghazi
(Euhesperides)

CYRENAICA

■ Province capital
● Other settlement
• Modern town
– – – Province boundary
— Roman road
Aswan Modern name
(Syene) Ancient name

Feet
3250
1625
650
0
Below sea level

◁ This portrait of a lady was painted on the outside of a wooden mummy case. Note her elaborate hair-style, make-up, earrings and necklace.

▽ A rich householder in Pompeii had this mosaic made, showing some of the wildlife on the banks of the Nile.

Mediterranean Sea

CRETA inset

Scale 1:3 500 000

0 — 80km

0 — 40 miles

Kastelli (Cisamum)
Khania (Cydonia)
(Phoenix)
(Cnossus)
(Chersonesus)
(Itanus)
Ierapetra (Hierapytna)
CRETA
(Gortyn)

Main map

(Paraetonium)

(Canopus)
Alexandria
(Sais)
(Sebennytus)
(Thmuis)
(Naucratis)
(Pelusium)
El-Arish (Rhinocolura)

(Comarum)

(Terenuthis)

(Heliopolis)
(Babylon)
Cairo
(Clysma)

(Memphis)

QATTARA
DEPRESSION

FAIYUM

(Dionysias)
(Arsinoe)

(Heracleopolis)

AEGYPTUS

ARABIAN
DESERT

Scale 1:4 000 000

0 — 200km

0 — 150 miles

(Oxyrhynchus)

Nile

Gulf of Suez

El Ashmunein (Hermopolis)
(Antinoopolis)

Red Sea

(Antaeopolis)

El Manshah (Ptolemais Hermiou)

(Coptos)

Luxor (Thebae)

Isna (Latopolis)
Nile
(Apollinopolis Magna)

Kom Ombo (Ombos)

Aswan (Syene)
(Philae)

GLOSSARY

Amphitheater Really means "theater in the round" because of its oval shape. This was where gladiators fought.

Amphora A huge pottery jar used to transport and store olive oil, wine and fish sauce.

Aqueduct Channel that brought water into the towns and cities, sometimes raised high up on arches to cross rivers or ravines.

Barbari Literally means "barbarians". The Romans used the name for anyone who was not Roman or did not speak Latin.

Basilica A long building with aisles, used as a public hall mainly for ceremonies and law courts.

Censor An elected official who kept register of all Roman citizens.

Centurion A soldier in charge of about 80 to 100 men in the Roman army. His rank was similar to a sergeant today.

Colonia A town of retired soldiers and their families set up in the provinces.

Consul The highest office a politician could hold in the Republic. Each year two consuls shared responsibility for the government, the army and the law courts.

Curia The name given to the building where the senate met to discuss public affairs.

Diocese The name given by the Emperor Diocletian to his 12 areas of government throughout the Empire.

Emperor *Imperator* in Latin; this was the title adopted by the Emperor Augustus. An emperor held supreme power in the Roman state.

Forum Originally, the open market place in a Roman town (the Greeks called it the *agora*). Most important public buildings were grouped in and around the forum.

Gladiators Warriors who fought bouts to the death in the amphitheater. They wore armor of different kinds.

Hypocaust The system used to heat floors and walls of buildings, mainly the baths. Hot air from a fire flowed under raised floors and through pipes in the walls.

Insula Literally means "island" and was the name for a block of buildings, surrounded by streets, in a town.

Legatus The title used by the commander of a legion and the governor of a province.

Legion The main unit in the Roman army. Usually made up of about 5,500 Roman citizens in the 1st century AD.

Mosaic A floor (sometimes a wall) made up of many fragments (called *tesserae*) of stone, tile or glass. Polished smooth, it made a picture or design.

Odeum A small theater used for concerts and recitals.

Orator A lawyer or politician well known for making public speeches.

Papyrus The Roman "paper" made from the stems of a water plant of the same name.

Patricians The nobles, or upper class, of Roman society.

Plebeians The name given to the ordinary working people of Roman society.

Praetors The officials elected as judges in the Roman state.

Procurators People appointed to look after the finances in the provinces. Some might be governors of small provinces.

Provinces Areas taken over and governed by the Romans. Italy, for example, was a province of Rome.

Quaestors Officials voted in to be in charge of all the state's finances – the treasury.

Republic The word the Romans used for their state with its elected officials and government.

Senate A large group of ex-officials who formed a type of "parliament" in Rome. They discussed public affairs and advised the elected officials such as the consuls.

Thermae The Latin word for the public baths, with their sweating room (*caldarium*) and sauna (*laconicum*).

Toga The outer garment (a large semicircular piece of cloth) which could only be worn by a citizen, therefore a man.

Villa A farming estate as well as a house in the country or by the seaside.

FURTHER READING

Reference books about the Romans
Ian Andrews, *Pompeii* (Lerner) 1978
Peter Connolly, *The Roman Army* (Silver Burdett) 1975
Peter Connolly, *Hannibal and the Enemies of Rome* (Silver Burdett) 1975
Mike Corbishley, *The Roman World* (Watts) 1986
Barbara Cork and Struan Reid, *The Young Scientist Book of Archaeology* (EDC Publishing) 1984
L.A. and J.A. Hamey, *The Roman Engineers* (Lerner) 1981
Peter Hodge (ed.) *Roman Technology and Crafts* (Aspects of Roman Life Series, Longman) 1979
David Macauley, *City: A Story of Roman Planning and Construction* (Houghton Mifflin) 1983

Stories about the Romans
Hans Baumann, *I marched with Hannibal* (Oxford) 1961

Rosemary Sutcliff, *Frontier Wolf* (E.P. Dutton) 1980
Rosemary Sutcliff, *The Eagle of the Ninth* (Oxford) 1954

Reference books for adults
Tim Cornell and John Matthews, *Atlas of the Roman World* (Facts On File) 1982
Kevin Greene, *The Archaeology of the Roman Economy* (Batsford) 1986
Naphtali Lewis and Meyer Reinhold (eds.), *Roman Civilization Sourcebook I: The Republic; II: The Empire* (Harper and Row) 1966 – translations from Roman writers and inscriptions.
Jane McIntosh, *The Practical Archaeologist* (Facts On File) 1986
Fergus Millar, *The Roman Empire and its Neighbors* (2nd Ed. Holmes and Meier) 1981
Richard Talbert (ed.), *Atlas of Classical History* (Macmillan) 1985

GAZETTEER

The gazetteer lists place names found on the maps. Each place has a separate entry including a page and grid reference number. For example:

Ad Aras 57 B2

Sometimes a modern place also has an ancient name form. This name is added to the entry before the reference number. For example:

Aleppo (Beroea) 87 B5

Abergavenny (Gobarrium) 67 B1
Ad Aras 57 D2
Adamclisi (Tropaeum Traiani) 75 G2
Adramyttium 80 A3
Aedepsus 77 C2
Aegae 77 C3
Aezania 80 B3
Agen (Aginnum) 61 B2
Aguntum 74 B3
Aîme (Axima) 61 C2
Aix-en-Provence (Aquae Sextiae) 61 C1
Akhisar (Thyatira) 80 B3
Alba Iulia (Apulum) 75 E3
Alcantara 56 B2
Alcester (Alauna) 67 C1
Aldborough (Isurium) 67 C3
Aleppo (Beroea) 87 B5
Alexandria 91 E4
Alexandria ad Issum 87 B5
Alfaro (Graccuris) 57 D4
Algiers (Icosium) 52 C4
Alicante (Lucentum) 57 D2
Almaden (Sisapo) 57 C2
Alvona 74 B3
Amasea 81 D4
Amastris 81 C4
Amathus 81 D1
Ambracia 77 B2
Amiens (Samarobriva) 61 B4
Amman (Philadelphia) 87 A1
Amphipolis 77 C3
Anazarbus 81 D2
Ancona 11 C4
Angers (Iuliomagus) 61 A3
Angoulême (Iculisma) 61 B2
Angustia 75 F3
Ankara (Ancyra) 81 C3
Annaba (Hippo Regius) 53 D4
Antaeopolis 91 F2
Antakya (Antiochia) 87 B5
Antalya (Attaleia) 80 C2
Antequera (Anticaria) 57 C1
Anthedon 77 C2
Antibes (Antipolis) 61 C1
Antinoopolis 87 C5
Antinoopolis 91 F2
Antiochia 80 C3
Apamea 87 B4
Aphrodisias 80 B2
Aphrodisias 75 F1
Apollinopolis Magna 91 G1
Apollonia 77 A3
Apri (Theodosiopolis) 75 G1
Aquae Regiae 53 E3
Araquil (Araceli) 57 D4
Archar (Ratiaria) 75 E2
Arezzo 11 B4
Argenton (Argentomagus) 61 B3
Argos 77 C1

Arixa (Arcobriga) 57 D3
Arles (Arelate) 61 C1
Arlon (Orolaunum) 61 C4
Arsinoe 91 F3
Ascalon 87 A2
Asine 77 C1
Asopus 77 C1
Aspendus 80 C2
Apsorus 74 B2
Astorga (Asturica Augusta) 56 B4
Aswan (Syene) 91 G1
Ataniya (Adana) 81 D2
Athens (Athenae) 77 C1
Auch (Elimberris) 61 B1
Augsburg (Augusta Vindelicorum) 74 A4
Augst (Augusta Rauricorum) 61 C3
Aureus Mons 75 D2
Autun (Augustodunum) 61 C3
Auxerre (Autessiodurum) 61 B3
Avallon (Aballo) 61 B3
Avila (Avela) 57 C3
Avranches (Legedia) 61 A4
Aydin (Tralles) 80 B2

Baalbek (Heliopolis) 87 B3
Babylon 91 F4
Baden-Baden (Aquae) 61 D4
Barca 90 A5
Barcelona (Barcino) 57 E3
Bari 11 D3
Bath (Aquae Sulis) 67 B1
Bayeux (Augustodurum) 61 A4
Bayonne (Lapurdum) 61 A1
Bazas (Vasates) 61 A2
Beauvais (Caesaromagus) 61 B4
Beersheba (Berosaba) 87 A2
Beirut (Berytus) 87 A3
Beja (Pax Iulia) 56 B2
Bejaia (Saldae) 53 D4
Belgrade (Singidunum) 75 D2
Benghazi (Euhesperides) 90 A5
Bergama (Pergamum) 80 B3
Bergamo 11 B5
Bergidum 56 B4
Berne 10 A6
Beroea 77 C3
Besançon (Besontio) 61 C3
Bethlehem 87 A2
Beziers (Baeterrae) 61 B1
Bilbilis 57 D3
Biskra (Vescera) 53 D3
Bistue Nova 74 C2
Bitola (Heraclea Lyncestis) 77 B3
Bitterne (Clausentum) 67 C1
Bizerte (Hippo Diarrhytus) 53 E4
Bodrum (Halicarnassus) 80 B2
Bologna 11 B5
Bonn (Bonna) 61 C5
Bordeaux (Burdigala) 61 A2
Boulogne (Gesoriacum) 61 B5
Bourges (Avaricum) 61 B3
Bowes (Lavatrae) 67 C3
Bowness (Maia) 66 E5, 67 B3
Braga (Bracara Augusto) 56 B3
Brancaster (Branodunium) 67 D2
Bregenz (Brigantium) 74 A3
Brescia 11 B5
Bressuire (Segora) 61 A3
Brindisi 11 D3
Brough (Petuaria) 67 C2
Brough (Verterae) 67 B3
Brza Palanka (Egeta) 75 E2
Bubon 80 B2
Budapest (Aquincum) 74 D3

Burnam 74 C2
Bursa (Prusa) 80 B4
Buseire (Circesium) 87 D4
Busra (Bostra) 87 B3
Buxton (Aquae Arnemetiae) 67 C2

Cabeza de Griego (Segobriga) 57 D2
Caceres (Norba) 56 B2
Cadiz (Gadez) 56 B1
Caeleon (Isca) 67 B1
Caernarvon (Segontium) 67 A2
Caerwent (Venta) 67 B1
Caesarea Maritima 87 A3
Caesarea Paneas 87 A3
Cagliari 11 B2
Cahors (Divona) 61 B2
Cairo 91 F3
Caister (Venta) 67 D2
Calahorra (Calagurris) 57 D4
Cambrai (Camaracum) 61 B5
Cambridge (Durolipons) 67 D2
Canopus 91 F4
Canterbury (Durovernum) 67 D1
Carcassonne (Carcaso) 61 B1
Carlisle (Luguvalium) 66 F5, 67 B3
Carmarthen (Moridunum) 67 A1
Carnutum 74 C4
Carpasia 81 D1
Cartagena (Carthago Nova) 57 D1
Carvoran (Magnis) 66 F5
Casablanca 52 A2
Casei (Samum) 75 E3
Castel Roussilion (Ruscino) 61 B1
Castlesteads 66 F5
Castra Traiana 75 F3
Catania 11 D1
Catterick (Cataractonium) 67 C3
Celei (Sucidava) 75 F2
Celje (Celeia) 74 C3
Chalon-sur-Saône (Cavillonum) 61 C3
Chartres (Autricum) 61 B4
Chelmsford (Caesaromagus) 67 D1
Cherbourg (Coriallum) 61 A4
Cherchell (Iol Caesarea) 52 C4
Chersonesus 91 I6
Chester (Deva) 67 B2
Chesterholm (Vindolanda) 66 F5
Chesters (Cilurnum) 66 F6
Chichester (Noviomagus) 67 C1
Cimiez (Cemenelum) 61 C1
Cirencester (Corinium) 67 C1
Cissa 74 C2
Claudiopolis 81 C4
Claudiopolis 81 D2
Clermont-Ferrand (Augustonemetum) 61 B2
Clysma 91 G4
Cnossus 91 I6
Cohors Breucorum 52 C3
Coimbra (Aeminium) 56 B3
Colchester (Camulodunum) 67 D1
Comama 80 C2
Comana Pontica 81 E4
Comarum 91 E4
Constantine (Cirta) 53 D4
Coptos 91 G2
Corbridge (Corstopitum) 66 F5, 67 B3
Cordoba (Corduba) 57 C1
Corfu (Corcyra) 77 A2
Corinium 74 C2
Corinth (Corinthus) 77 C1

Cucusus 81 E3
Cumidava 75 F3
Cuprija (Horreum Margi) 75 E2
Curicum 74 B3
Curium 81 C1
Cyaneae 80 B2
Cyme 80 A3
Cyrrhus 87 B5
Cyzicus 80 B4

Damascus 87 B3
Danaba 87 B4
Decize (Decetia) 61 B3
Delminium 74 C2
Delphi 77 C2
Demetrias 77 C2
Denia (Dianium) 57 E2
Derna (Darnis) 90 B5
Deultum 75 G2
Diana Veteranorum 53 D3
Digne (Dinia) 61 C2
Dijon (Diblo) 61 C3
Dinar (Celaenae) 80 C3
Dionysias 91 F3
Diospolis 87 A2
Dium 77 C3
Djemila (Cuicul) 53 D4
Dodona 77 B2
Dorchester (Durnovaria) 67 B1
Dorchester (Durnovaria) 67 C1
Doriscus 75 F1
Dougga (Thugga) 53 E4
Dover (Dubris) 67 D1
Droitwich (Salinae) 67 B2
Drumburgh (Congavata) 66 E5
Dunakömlöd (Lussonium) 74 D3
Dura-Europus 87 D4
Durostorum 75 D2
Durrës (Epidamnus) 77 A3

Ebchester (Vindomora) 67 G5
Ecija (Astigi) 57 C1
Edirne (Hadrianopolis) 75 F1
El Ashmunein (Hermopolis) 91 F2
El Asnam (Castellum Tingitanum) 52 C4
El Jem (Thysdrus) 53 E3
El Kantara (Calceus Herculis) 53 D3
El Kef (Sicca Veneria) 53 E4
El Manshah (Ptolemais Hermiou) 91 F2
el Padron (Iria Elavia) 56 B4
El Qanawat (Canatha) 87 B3
El-Arish (Rhinocolura) 91 G4
Elaeusa 81 D2
Elat (Aila) 87 A2
Eleusis 77 C2
Embrun (Eburodurum) 61 C2
Epfach (Abudiacum) 74 A3
Ephesus 80 B2
Eregli (Heraclea Pontica) 81 C4
Erythrae 80 A3
Eskishehir (Dorylaeum) 80 C3
Estrées-sur-Noye 61 B4
Eupatoria 81 E4
Evora (Ebora) 56 B2
Exeter (Isca) 67 B1

Faro (Ossonoba) 56 B1
Ferrara 11 B5
Fès 52 A3
Feurs (Forum Segusiavorcum) 61 C2
Fishbourne 67 C1
Florence 11 B4
Foggia 11 D3
Forlì 11 C5
Fréjus (Forum Iulii) 61 C1

Gabès (Tacapae) 53 E2
Gafsa (Capsa) 53 E3
Gangra 81 D4
Garsaura 81 D3
Gaza 87 A2
Gazipasa (Selinus) 81 C2
Geneva 61 C3
Genoa 11 A5
Geraestus 77 D1
Gerona (Gerunda) 57 E3
Gibraltar (Calpe) 57 C1
Gijon (Gigia) 57 C4
Gloucester (Glevum) 67 B1
Godmanchester (Durovigutum) 67 C2
Gorsium 74 D3
Gortyn 91 I6
Grenoble (Cularo) 61 C2
Guadix (Acci) 57 C1
Györ (Arrabona) 74 C3

Haidra (Ammaedara) 53 E3
Halae 77 C2
Halton (Onnum) 66 G6
Hama (Epiphania) 87 B4
Harran (Carrhae) 87 C5
Hebron 87 A2
Hedum 74 D2
Heliopolis 91 F4
Hephaestia 77 D2
Heracleia 75 G2
Heracleopolis 91 F3
Herodion 87 A2
High Rochester (Aquae Sulis) 67 B3
Homs (Emesa) 87 B4
Housesteads (Vercovicium) 66 F6
Huercal (Urci) 57 D1
Huesca (Osca) 57 D4

Iader 74 C2
Ierapetra (Hierapytna) 91 J6
Ilchester (Lindinis) 67 B1
Inchtuthil (Victoria) 67 B3
Inebolu (Abonuteichus) 81 D4
Innsbruk (Veldidena) 74 A3
Inveresk (Coria) 67 B3
Isaura 81 C2
Isna (Latopolis) 91 G1
Issus 81 E2
Istanbul (Byzantium) 75 G1
Isthmia 77 C1
Italica 56 B1
Itanus 91 J6
Izmir (Smyrna) 80 B3
Izmit (Nicomedia) 80 B4
Iznik (Nicaea) 80 B4

Jarash (Gerasa) 87 A3
Jericho 87 A1
Jerusalem (Aelia Capitolina) 87 A2
Jijel (Igilgili) 53 D4

Kadiköy (Chalcedon) 80 B4
Kaliste (Municipium) 75 E2
Karaman (Laranda) 81 D2
Karnak (Characmoba) 87 A2
Karpuzu (Alinda) 80 B2
Kastelli (Cisamum) 91 H6
Kavalla (Neapolis) 77 D3
Kayseri (Mazaca) 81 D3
Kenchela (Mascula) 53 D3
Kenchester (Magnis) 67 B2
Khamissa (Thubursicu Numidarum) 53 D4
Khania (Cydonia) 91 I6
Koblenz (Confluentes) 61 C5

93

Köln (Colonia Agrippina) 61 C5
Kom Ombo (Ombos) 91 G1
Komotini (Porsule) 75 F1
Konstanz (Constantia) 74 A3
Konya (Iconium) 81 C2
Kostolac (Viminacium) 75 E2

La Coruna (Brigantium) 56 B4
La Spezia 11 B5
Lambese (Lambaesis) 53 D3
Laodicea 87 A4
Lapithos (Lapethus) 81 D1
Lapseki (Lampsacus) 80 A4
Larisa 77 C2
Larnaca (Citium) 81 D1
Le Mans (Suindinum) 61 B3
Lectoure (Lactora) 61 B1
Leicester (Ratae) 67 C2
Leiva (Libia) 57 C4
Lejjun 87 A3
Léon (Legio) 57 C4
Leptis Magna 53 F2
Lerida (Ilerda) 57 E3
Levadhia (Lebadea) 77 C2
Lezuza (Libisosa) 57 D2
Limenia 81 C1
Limoges (Augustoritum) 61 B2
Lincoln (Lindum) 67 C2
Lind (Ad Pontem) 74 B3
Lisbon (Olisipo) 56 A2
Lisieux (Noviomagus) 61 B4
Lissus 75 D1
Littlechester (Derventio) 67 C2
Lixus 52 A3
Lodève (Luteva) 61 B1
London (Londinium) 67 C1
Lorch (Lauriacum) 74 B4
Lovech (Melta) 75 F2
Lugo (Lucus Augusti) 56 B4
Luxor (Thebae) 91 G1
Lyon (Lugdunum) 61 C2

Madaba 87 A2
Madrid 57 C3
Magnum 74 C2
Mahón (Mago) 57 E2
Maienfeld (Magia) 74 A3
Mainz (Moguntiacum) 61 D5
Malaga (Malaca) 57 C1
Malatya (Melitene) 81 E3
Maluesa 75 D2
Manchester (Mamucium) 67 B2
Mangalia (Callatis) 75 G2
Mantinea 77 C1
Marathon 77 C2
Marcianopolis 75 G2
Marrakech 52 A1
Marsa Susah (Apollonia) 90 A5
Marseille (Massilia) 61 C1
Martos (Tucci) 57 C1
Masada 87 A2
Mautern (Faviana) 74 C4
Medellin (Metellinum) 56 C2
Megalopolis 77 C1
Mehadia (Ad Mediam) 75 E2
Melilla (Rusaddir) 52 B3
Membij (Hierapolis) 87 B5
Memphis 91 F3
Merida (Emerita Augusta) 56 B2
Mertola (Myrtilis) 56 B1
Mesa de Asta (Hasta) 56 B1
Messad (Castellum Dimmidi) 52 C3
Messina 11 D2
Messini (Messene) 77 B1
Metropolis 77 B2
Metz (Divodurum) 61 C4
Milan 11 B5
Mitrovica (Sirmium) 75 D2
Moigrad (Porolissum) 75 E3

Montana 75 E2
Montoro (Epora) 57 C2
Mostaganem 52 C3
Moutiers (Darantasia) 61 C2
Mycenae 77 C1
Myra 80 B2
Mytilene 80 A3

Nabeul (Neapolis) 53 E4
Nantes (Portus Namnetum) 61 A3
Naples 11 C3
Narbonne (Narbo) 61 B1
Narona 74 C2
Naryca 77 C2
Naucratis 91 F4
Naupactus 77 B2
Naxos 77 D1
Nazareth 87 A3
Neapolis 87 A3
Nefta (Nepete) 53 E2
Néris-les-Bains (Aquae Neri) 61 B3
Nesebur (Mesembria) 75 G2
Nessana 87 A2
Netherby (Castra Exploratorum) 66 F6, 67 B3
Neuburg (Submuntorium) 74 A4
Neuss (Novaesium) 61 C5
Newcastle (Pons Aelius) 67 C3, 67 G5
Newstead (Trimontium) 67 B3
Nicopolis 77 B2
Nicopolis 81 E4
Nicopolis ad Istrum 75 F2
Nicopolis ad Nestum 75 E1
Nijmegen (Noviomagus) 61 C5
Nijon (Noviomagus) 61 C4
Nîmes (Nemausus) 61 C1
Nis (Naissus) 75 E2
Nizy (Minatiacum) 61 C4
Novae 75 F2
Nusaybin (Nisibis) 87 D5
Nyons (Noviodunum) 61 C3

Oboda 87 A2
Oenoanda 80 B2
Oescus 75 F2
Ohrid (Lychnidus) 77 A3
Olbasa 80 B2
Old Sarum (Sorviodunum) 67 C1
Olympia 77 B1
Oporto (Oportus Cale) 56 B3
Oppidum Novum 52 A3
Oran (Portus Magnus) 52 B3
Orange (Arausio) 61 C2
Oretum 57 C2
Oricum 77 A3
Osijek (Mursa) 74 D3
Osma (Uxama Argela) 57 C3
Osuna (Urso) 57 C1
Oudna (Uthina) 53 E4
Oviedo (Ovetum) 57 C4
Oxyrhynchus 91 F3

Padua 11 B5
Palanka (Lederata) 75 E2
Palencia (Pallantia) 57 C4
Palermo 11 C2
Palma 57 E2
Palmyra 87 C4
Pamplona (Pompaelo) 57 D4
Pamukkale (Hierapolis) 80 B2
Paphus 81 C1
Paraetonium 91 D4
Paris (Lutetia) 61 B4
Parma 11 B5
Passau (Castra Batava) 74 B4
Passau-Instadt (Boiodurum) 74 B4

Patras (Patrae) 77 B2
Pecs (Sopianae) 74 D3
Pella 77 C3
Pelusium 91 G4
Périgueux (Vesunna) 61 B2
Perinthus 75 G1
Perugia 11 C4
Pescara 11 C4
Pessinus 81 C3
Petra 87 A2
Pevensey (Anderita) 67 D1
Philae 91 G1
Philippi 77 D3
Philippopolis (Plovdiv) 75 F2
Phoenix 91 I6
Piacenza 11 B5
Piraeus 77 C1
Pisa 11 B4
Podandus 81 D2
Poitiers (Limonum) 61 B3
Pollensa (Pollentia) 57 E2
Pons Aluti 75 F2
Portus Victoriae 57 C4
Potidaea 77 C3
Praetorium 75 F3
Priene 80 B2
Ptuj (Poetovio) 74 C3

Qirzah (Ghirza) 53 F1

Rabat 52 A3
Raqqa (Nic Horium) 87 C4
Raphanaea 87 B4
Ravenna 11 C5
Regensburg (Castra Regina) 74 B4
Reggio di Calabria 11 D2
Reims (Durocortorum) 61 C4
Rennes (Condate) 61 A4
Retortillo (Iuliobriga) 57 C4
Rhodes (Rhodus) 80 B2
Rhodiapolis 80 C2
Ribchester (Bremetennacum) 67 B2
Richborough (Rutupiae) 67 D1
Rimini 11 C5
Risafe (Resapha) 87 C4
Risinium 74 D2
Rochester (Durobrivae) 67 D1
Rochester (Vindovala) 67 G6
Rodez (Segodunum) 61 B2
Rom (Rauranum) 61 B3
Rome 11 C3
Rosenheim (Pons Aeni) 74 B3
Rouen (Rotomagus) 61 B4
Royan (Noviorigum) 61 A2
Rusucurru 53 C4

Sadouri (Ausum) 53 D3
Sagalassus 80 B2
Saguntum 57 D2
Saida (Sidon) 87 A3
Sais 91 F4
Salamanca (Salmantica) 57 C3
Salamis 81 D1
Salerno 11 C3
Salonae 74 C2
Saloniki (Thessalonica) 77 C3
Salvium 74 C2
Salzburg (Iuvavum) 74 B3
Sami (Same) 77 B2
Samothracia 77 D3
Samsat (Samosata) 87 C5
Samsun (Amisus) 81 E4
Santarem (Scallabis) 56 B2
Sarande (Onchesmus) 77 B2
Sardis 80 B3
Sarduc (Centum Putei) 75 E3
Sarmizegetusa 75 E3
Sasamon (Segisamo) 57 C4

Sassari 11 A3
Satala 81 F4
Sbeitla (Sufetula) 53 E3
Scardonia 74 C2
Scitarijevo (Andautonia) 74 C3
Scodra 75 D2
Scythopolis 87 A3
Sebennytus 91 F4
Sées (Seii) 61 B4
Segovia 57 C3
Selge 80 C2
Selimiye (Side) 81 C2
Senia 74 B3
Sens (Agedincum) 61 B4
Seriane 87 B4
Setif (Sitifis) 53 D4
Seville (Hispalis) 56 B1
Sfax (Taparura) 53 E3
Shahhat (Cyrene) 90 A5
Sicyon 77 C1
Side 81 E4
Siga 52 B3
Sigacik (Teos) 80 A3
Silchester (Calleva) 67 C1
Silifke (Seleucia) 81 D2
Simancas (Septimanca) 57 C3
Singara 87 D5
Sinop (Sinope) 81 D5
Sisak (Siscia) 74 C3
Sivas (Megalopolis) 81 E3
Skopje (Scupi) 75 E2
Sofia (Serdica) 75 E2
Soli 81 D2
Sousse (Hadrumetum) 53 E3
South Shields 67 G5
Sparti (Sparta) 77 C1
Speyer (Noviomagus) 61 D4
Split (Aspalathos) 74 C2
St Albans (Verulamium) 67 C1
St Rémy (Glanum) 61 C1
Stanwix 66 F5
Stara Zagora (Beroe) 75 F2
Stobi 77 B3
Strasbourg (Argentorate) 61 C4
Stratus 77 B2
Susa (Segusio) 61 C2
Synnada 80 C3
Szombathely (Savaria) 74 C3
Szöny (Brigetio) 74 D3

Tabarka (Thabraca) 53 E4
Tadcaster (Calcaria) 67 C2
Talavera la Vieja (Augustobriga) 57 C2
Tamassus 81 D1
Tangiers (Tingi) 52 A3
Taranto 11 D3
Tarazona (Turiasso) 57 D3
Tarragona (Tarraco) 57 E3
Tarsatica 74 B3
Tarsus 81 D2
Tavium 81 D3
Tebessa (Thevestis) 53 E3
Tel Aviv-Yafo (Joppa) 87 A3
Telmessus 80 B2
Telmine (Turris Tamallent) 53 E2
Ténès (Cartenna) 52 C4
Terenuthis 91 F4
Terni 11 C4
Teurnia 74 B3
Teuthrone 77 C1
Thamusida 52 A3
Thapsus 53 E3
Thasos 77 D3
Thebes (Thebae) 77 C2
Thera 77 D1
Thisvi (Thisbe) 77 C2
Thmuis 91 F4
Tiberias 87 A3
Tiklat (Tupusuctu) 53 D4

Timgad (Thamugadi) 53 D3
Tinos 77 D1
Tiranë 11 E3
Titulcia 57 C3
Tlemcen (Pomaria) 52 B3
Toledo (Toletum) 57 C2
Tongeren (Atuatuca) 61 C5
Tortosa (Dertosa) 57 E3
Toul (Tullum) 61 C4
Toulouse (Tolosa) 61 B1
Tournai (Turnacum) 61 B5
Tours (Caesarodunum) 61 B3
Towcester (Lactodorum) 67 C2
Trapezus 81 F4
Trier (Augusta Treverorum) 61 C4
Trieste 11 C5
Trikkala (Tricca) 77 B2
Tripoli (Oea) 53 F2
Tripoli (Tripolis) 87 A4
Troesmis 75 G3
Troezen 77 C1
Trogir (Tragurium) 74 C2
Troy (Ilium) 80 A3
Troyes (Augustobona) 61 C4
Tukrah (Tauchira) 90 A5
Tulln (Commagena) 74 C4
Tulmaythah (Ptolemais) 90 A5
Tunis (Carthago) 11 B1, 53 E4
Turin 10 A5
Turnu-Severin (Drobeta) 75 E2
Tyana 81 D2
Tyre (Tyrus) 87 A3

Ulmetum 75 G2
Ulpia Traiana Sarmizegetusa 75 E3
Ulpianum 75 E2
Um Qeis (Gadara) 87 A3
Urfa (Edessa) 87 C5
Utique (Utica) 53 E4
Uzès (Ucetia) 61 C2

Valencia (Valentia) 57 D2
Valkenburg 61 C6
Varna (Odessus) 75 G2
Venice 11 C5
Verona 11 B5
Vevey (Viviscus) 61 C3
Vicenza 11 B5
Vich (Ausa) 57 E3
Vienna (Vindobona) 74 C4
Vienne (Vienna) 61 C2
Villach (Santicum) 74 B3
Vinkovci (Cibalae) 74 D3
Virunum 74 B3
Vize (Bizye) 75 F1

Wallsend (Segedunum) 67 C3, 67 G5
Water Newton (Durobrivae) 67 C2
Weisbaden (Aquae Mattiacae) 61 D5
Wels (Ovilava) 74 B4
Willoughby (Vernemetum) 67 C2
Winchester (Venta) 67 C1
Windisch (Vindonissa) 61 D3
Worms (Borbetomagus) 61 D4
Wroxeter (Viroconium) 67 B2

Xanten (Vetera) 61 C5
Xanthus 80 B2

York (Eburacum) 67 C2

Zamora (Ocelum Duri) 57 C3
Zaragoza (Caesaraugusta) 57 D3
Zeugma 87 B5
Zintan (Tentheos) 53 F2
Zuccabar 52 A3

INDEX